Knead It, Punch It, Bake It!

Dear Daniel —
There is nothing more
wonderful than
creating something —
I hope you'll always
create great things —
Here is a guide to
the adventures of
bread making — Follow
it carefully as you
create great things —
Love,
Mommy
Hanukkah
1998

Knead It, Punch It, Bake It!

The Ultimate Breadmaking Book for Parents and Kids

Judith and Evan Jones

Illustrations by Mitra Modarressi

Houghton Mifflin Company

Boston New York

For information about permission to reproduce selections from this book, write to Permissions, Houghton Mifflin Company, 215 Park Avenue South, New York, New York 10003.

Library of Congress Cataloging-in-Publication Data
Jones, Judith.
Knead it, punch it, bake it!: the ultimate breadmaking book for parents and kids / Judith and Evan Jones: illustrations by Mitra Modarressi.—2nd ed.
p. cm.
Includes index.
Summary: Presents more than forty recipes for baking all kinds and shapes of bread from French bread to peanut butter muffins to pizza.
ISBN 0-395-89256-2
1. Bread—Juvenile literature. [1. Bread.] I. Jones, Evan, date. II. Modarressi, Mitra, III. Title.
TX769.J65 1998
641.8'15—dc21
98-27319   CIP AC

Printed in the United States of America
Cover illustration by Mitra Modarressi
Book design by Susan McClellan

BP 10 9 8 7 6 5 4 3 2 1

For Bronwyn and Alex and Matt

ACKNOWLEDGMENTS

Thanks to all the young people who helped test the new recipes for this second edition—Heather Floody, Nathan Floody, Holly Nagel, Larry David, J. P. Rooney, Josy Norton, Jackson Norton, and Tayo Norton. They were great bakers and tasters.

The book would not have had its second life were it not for the vision of the gifted editor Rux Martin. She has been full of good ideas, and *Knead It, Punch It, Bake It!* has been greatly enhanced by her special touch.

Mitra Modarressi has made an invaluable contribution to this edition with her delightful drawings, and she has been a pleasure to work with.

■ Contents ■

PREFACE TO THE NEW EDITION

In the seventeen years since this book was first published, fewer and fewer people have been doing any real cooking at home. Now, more often than not, fast food is just heated up or the family goes out to grab a snack. The kitchen has become a forlorn place with no lovely sounds of batter being beaten in a bowl or vegetables chopped on a board, no heady smells coming from the oven of a chicken roasting or bread baking. People say they don't have time to cook anymore. But what are they saving all that time for? What they don't realize is that they are depriving themselves of one of the greatest pleasures in life.

You have only to invite some children into your kitchen to make bread together to realize the genuine joy there is to be found in cooking. Particularly in breadmaking. Youngsters aren't a bit afraid of the idea of dealing with yeast and of kneading, all of which seems to scare off timid adult cooks. They just plunge right in, toss the dough around, watch it mysteriously rise in the bowl, and have fun punching it down again and fashioning it into different shapes and breathing in the seductive aroma as the loaves bake in the oven. To say nothing of the final reward in tearing open a warm, crusty loaf and recognizing for the first time what really good homemade bread tastes like. So let's get the children to lead us back to the kitchen, and let's all break bread together again.

People often ask me at what age children should start baking. I feel they're never too young. Last summer when I was testing some of the new recipes for this book, I invited a few children over to help in our kitchen in Vermont. The youngest was my two-and-a-half-year-old grandnephew Tayo, and he immediately pulled up a chair and climbed up on it, dipped his hands in flour, and started kneading the dough. After that step was finished, I told him the dough was tired now and needed a rest, so he carefully put the dough in the bowl and covered it up with a towel, and we tiptoed away. I also told him that while the dough was napping it was going to grow—in fact, that it was going to grow so fast that when we came back after lunch it would be swelling up over the top of the bowl. He could scarcely believe it when we returned an hour later and he pulled off the cover and saw the magic with his own eyes.

We were making pitas that day, and Tayo loved punching down the sleep-swollen dough, pinching off small pieces, and turning each around and around in his little hands to form a golf ball. When it came to rolling the balls out into circles, he grabbed my big rolling pin and insisted on doing the job himself. Later, when these disks of dough were in the oven and we peeked to see that they had puffed up into balloon shapes, he was beside himself with pleasure and announced, his face dusted with flour, "I am a BAKER!"

The pitas we were testing are typical of the kinds of breads from different parts of the world that we are all enjoying today and that we wanted to include in this new edition. We also have a recipe for pita's Indian cousin, the naan, and for the current big favorite, the bagel. All of these breads are fun to stuff or spread with a topping to give you a new kind of sandwich. Then there are the offshoots of pizza—focaccia, which can be dressed with different toppings, and calzones, filled and baked with a tasty stuffing.

When one thinks of bread, one thinks of a good breakfast, and we have included some delicious new recipes for English muffins, sticky buns, scones, a seeded loaf, baking powder biscuits, and doughnuts that are baked instead of deep-fried. And don't miss the long, thin bread sticks and soft, salt-encrusted pretzels, always a big hit at parties.

All the old favorites are here, too, that youngsters we worked with seventeen years ago are still baking today. Once you get hooked on breadbaking, it's hard to stop. And you'll always find time. For one thing, it is a relaxing pastime. While the dough is rising, or later when it's baking, you can go off and watch television or do homework or take a swim. And, believe me, when the result of your labors is on the table, you'll really feel proud of your accomplishment. So gather some friends together and get started. You might even seduce the members of the older generation, who never have time to cook, into joining in the fun.

Judith Jones
1998

Necessary Baking Equipment

- Bowls (small, medium, large)
- A set of metal or plastic measuring cups with handles for dry ingredients (¼, ⅓, ½, 1 cup), see page 18
- A glass measuring cup with a spout for liquid ingredients (1- or 2-cup size), see page 19
- One or two large wooden mixing spoons
- Rubber spatula
- Dough scraper (or a painter's scraper will do)
- Kitchen towel
- Roll of plastic wrap
- Roll of waxed paper
- Pot holders or mitts
- Two 8-inch loaf pans
- One 9-inch loaf pan
- Two baking sheets
- One 8-inch square baking pan
- Two 8-inch cake pans (for Sticky Buns)
- A muffin tin of 10 cups or two tins of 6-8 cups each
- One 10-inch tube pan or Bundt pan (for Bubble Bread)
- Cast-iron frying pan
- Cooling rack
- Pastry brush
- Four-sided grater
- Knives—one small paring knife, one large knife, one bread knife
- Vegetable peeler
- Kitchen timer

Optional—

*or What to Ask For
for Your Birthday When
You've Become a REAL Baker*

- French Bread pans
- Baking stone or tiles to line the oven rack, see page 65
- Pizza paddle
- Soapstone griddle, see page 65
- A chef's hat

INTRODUCTION

There's an old saying in the valleys north of the Persian Gulf that bread is older than man. In fact, farmers in Sumeria were harvesting barley and wheat at least ten thousand years ago, and the grain was turned into primitive bread that was baked on hot stones in open fires.

A couple of thousand years later, in the Nile Valley of Egypt, the oven was invented and the process of leavening (making a dough that rises) was perfected. Egyptian bakers discovered that a mixture of wheat and water, when left long enough in a warm place, would start to bubble and froth—in other words, it became fermented. By kneading some of this live, gassy liquid into a bread dough, they found that the dough would swell up as it became honeycombed with tiny air pockets.

When this risen dough was formed into loaves and baked, the texture of the bread was much lighter and the flavor was better. Thus it wasn't long before the Egyptians were making fifty kinds of bread with various shapes and flavors, and bread became so important to them that it was even prepared to accompany the dead on their journeys to the hereafter. (Archaeologists opening a royal tomb in 1936 found several loaves thirty-five centuries— that's 3,500 years—old.)

Basically, breadmaking has changed very little since the ancient dwellers along the Nile developed the leavening process. The big difference is that today we have learned to capture that live fermentation in the form of yeast and to seal it in a package. When we add this captured yeast to warm liquid, it springs to life again. The softened yeast is mixed into bread dough and starts feeding on the starch in the dough, making it swell as the healthy gases expand inside. The process seems mysterious—and that's half the fun. There is no other experience quite like making a dough that puffs up and turns into a plump, golden loaf of bread.

Incidentally, if you are making a yeast bread for the first time, you should start with Basic White Bread on page 20, because there all the techniques and variables are spelled out.

When you first plunge your hands into the dough, your fingers come out all sticky. But as you work in a little more flour and start folding, pushing, and turning the dough—the process known as kneading—you distribute the fermenting yeast cells all through the dough. Then, as the yeast cells start to expand, the dough becomes elastic—alive and bouncy. Making bread is exciting. As you work with the dough, you can feel it changing. You can watch as the yeast in the dough forms the tiny air pockets that make it rise. You can see it collapse as you punch it down again to form loaves of different shapes.

When the dough in the loaf pans swells up again over the tops of the pans, you know it is time for baking, and you pop the pans into a hot oven. As the bread you have made bakes behind the oven door, your kitchen fills with wonderful smells. Then at last you have the pleasure of slicing the resilient crust, inhaling the fragrance of the bread, and biting into your own delicious-tasting fresh loaf.

Introduction

All About Yeast

Yeast is a living substance that is in the air, on the leaves of trees, in their bark, in the skin of fruits, and in the soil. We could capture it and get a fermentation going that would then feed on the flour in a bread dough and make it rise. But that is tricky, and the results are unpredictable. Fortunately we have readily available in the supermarket today a cultivated yeast that has been dehydrated. All that is needed to bring it back to life is to dissolve it in warm water. Then it is ready to go to work on the flour, to feed on it and give off the carbon dioxide and alcohol that make the dough swell and rise.

How hot is warm? The water you dissolve the yeast in should be warm but not hot. If the water is too hot, it kills the yeast. So how do you tell if it's too hot? The best way is to stick your very clean finger deep into the water and hold it there. If you can keep it there comfortably, you'll know the temperature of the water is fine.

Supermarket yeast comes in small, foil-lined ½-ounce packets. But it is also available in bulk or in jars in some markets or health food stores, and if you do a lot of baking, it is well worth buying it in quantity. The ½-ounce packet is equal to slightly less than 1 tablespoon, so in our recipes we call for either 1 package or 1 scant tablespoon of active dry yeast, meaning just a little less than a full, leveled-off tablespoon. You don't need to be too exact.

(continued on page 18)

Always keep yeast in the refrigerator. The envelopes are marked with an expiration date. But if you have loose yeast in a jar and are not sure whether it has been around too long and is too old to do its work, you can test it by dissolving a tablespoon of it in ¼ cup warm water mixed with 1 teaspoon sugar. After several minutes, it should swell up a bit and look bubbly on the surface. You'll know then that it's still alive.

How to Measure

It is important to measure ingredients accurately. Dry ingredients, such as flour and sugar, are measured by dipping a metal or plastic measuring spoon or cup— whatever size is called for—into the dry ingredient and scooping it up, filled to the brim or even overflowing the brim, and then leveling it off by running a knife or spatula across the top.

Sometimes it is hard to remember which is the tablespoon and which is the teaspoon. Marion Cunningham, who wrote a wonderful book called *Cooking with Children,* has a good trick: remember, she says, that a table is big, whereas a teacup is much smaller.

For liquid ingredients, most people find it easier to use a glass measuring cup with a spout for easy pouring. You fill the cup to the measure called for and then hold the cup to eye level to make sure the amount you have poured in is level with the measure indicated on the cup.

The spout also makes pouring easier. But you don't need to be too fussy. If you prefer to use one of the set of metal cups with handles that have the amount marked on them, just do so, but use a good steady hand.

Butter is easy to measure because the measurements are marked on each ¼-pound stick of butter. A stick is ½ cup or 8 tablespoons, and you just lop off the amount you need as indicated on the foil or paper wrapping covering the stick.

A solid fat that comes in a can, such as vegetable shortening, is harder to measure. You have to spoon the fat out of the can and pack it into the measuring cup that is called for, pressing it down tightly and leveling off the top.

Basic White Bread

Makes two 8-inch-long loaves

*T*his basic formula will give you two light, faintly sweet loaves that swell up proudly in their baking pans and make nice generous slices for sandwiches and morning toast.

1	package (1 scant tablespoon) active dry yeast
¼	cup warm water
2½	cups milk
2	teaspoons salt
4	tablespoons (½ stick) butter or vegetable shortening
⅓	cup honey or sugar
6½ - 7	cups white flour

Put the yeast in a large bowl and pour the warm water over it. After a minute stir the yeast with your finger to make sure it is thoroughly dissolved and creamy-looking.

Heat 1 cup of the milk in a medium saucepan and stir in the salt, butter or shortening, and honey or sugar until dissolved. Turn off the heat, then stir in the remaining 1½ cups milk and let cool. When the mixture is cool enough that you can hold your finger in it, pour the contents of the pan into the bowl with the dissolved yeast. Stir with a big wooden spoon to mix well.

Start adding 6 cups of the flour, stirring with the spoon after you've added each cup. You'll notice by the sixth cup that the dough is getting hard to stir. At that point, scrape the bottom and sides of the bowl well with the spoon and turn the dough out onto a well-floured work surface. Let the dough rest while you clean out your bowl.

A Work Surface That's the Right Height

As a work surface, use a clean countertop or a large, smooth board; either one will prove helpful in kneading. If you're shorter than about five feet two inches, you may find it easier to knead on a table that is lower than the usual counter height. If there isn't a lower surface available, try standing on a chair or a stool. You want to be able to put your body into the motion of kneading, from the shoulders down. It's not just an exercise for the hands, so the work surface should be just a little higher than your waist—the thrust of kneading uses the force and weight of your shoulders and upper torso.

Now scrape the dough off to one side. Scoop up any scattered bits and pat them into the dough. Flour the surface again. Pick up the dough and slap it down on the floured area. This rough treatment will get the gluten in the flour to wake up and start doing its work. (Gluten is the plant protein in the flour that provides the elasticity.) Do this a few times, adding more flour as needed so the dough won't stick. Pat the dough into a ball and clean off your hands.

Flour your hands and knead. If your hands are small, you may find it hard to get the dough going in the beginning. If so, just slap it around a bit, using the dough scraper to get it up off the surface. Dust with flour and slap again. If there are two or more of you making bread, you can coat your hands with flour and toss the mass of dough back and forth like a big ball, folding it over after every catch. Very soon it will become less sticky, and you can

then knead it on the floured work surface.
To knead, pick up the far side of the
dough and pull it up and over toward you,
then press into it with the heels of your
hands, pushing it away from you. Turn
the dough clockwise a quarter of the
way around (so 12 o'clock is where 3 o'clock was)
and knead again. Repeat the kneading and
the turning of the dough, adding more
flour as necessary so it doesn't stick.
Don't tug at the dough and pull it apart;
keep it roughly ball-shaped.

Times required for kneading vary, depending
on the size and personality of the breadmakers.

Preheating the Oven

Most ovens take about 15 minutes to reach the temperature you set them for, so turn on your oven 15 minutes before the final rising of the dough has been accomplished. In other words, if your recipe calls for letting the formed loaves rise for about 45 minutes, turn on the oven after 30 minutes of that rising and it will be nice and hot—ready to receive the loaves—15 minutes later.

In the case of breads that don't have to rise and are simply mixed and then baked, start your oven before you do anything else.

A kitchen timer that you wind up and set is useful to help you keep track of the timing.

A towering man, using only one hand, can knead in half the time it might take an average ten-year-old on the first try. So be patient if the kneading goes faster for someone else—it is fun as long as it lasts.

The dough will become more and more elastic as the gluten develops. After 10 minutes or so of kneading, it will seem smooth and bouncy and will no longer stick to your hands or to the work surface. There may be a few air bubbles or blisters on the surface from the gas the yeast has created.

To test it, try plunging a couple of fingers into the center of the dough and removing them quickly; if the dough springs back, you'll know it has been kneaded enough.

(*continued on page 24*)

𝒴east ■ ℬreads

When the dough is ready, use a little soft butter or vegetable shortening—it doesn't matter which—to lightly grease the cleaned bowl. Put the dough in and turn it over to coat all sides with grease. Cover the bowl (plastic wrap is best because it seals in the moisture) and leave the dough to rise. The temperature of the kitchen is usually warm enough, but if it's particularly cold, put the bowl near the stove or a radiator. When the yeasty mass has risen to twice its original size, it will look swollen and rounded on top, and it will be very light and springy to the touch.

In about 1¼ hours, when you can see that the dough has grown to twice its original size (if it hasn't, leave it for another half hour or so), punch it down by giving it a good sock or two with your fist; you'll feel it deflating under you like air going out of a rubber tire.

Scrape the dough out of the bowl onto your floured surface again. Divide it in half. You want to shape each half to fit your loaf pan, so pat it into an oval approximately the pan's length. Ease and tuck the long sides under, shaping the dough gently, not tearing it or you will break its elastic skin. Pinch the seams together on the bottom side.

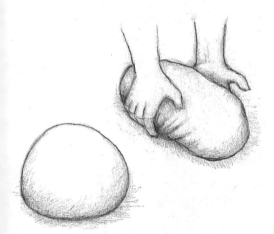

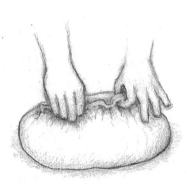

Lightly but thoroughly rub two standard 8-inch-long loaf pans with butter or vegetable shortening. Place the loaves inside, seam side down. The pans will be about two-thirds full, and if the loaves look a bit uneven, punch them lightly to even them out, but don't worry—a homemade loaf should have a homemade shape. Cover the pans loosely with a kitchen towel and let the dough rise again for about 50 minutes, or until it has swelled slightly over the tops of the pans. (continued on page 26)

Yeast ■ Breads

After about 35 minutes—15 minutes before the final rising time is up—preheat the oven to 350 degrees.

When the loaves are ready, put them in the oven and bake for 45 minutes. At that point the tops will have browned lightly. If you want to make sure the bottom is well cooked, too, remove one of the pans carefully with pot holders or mitts. Slip out the loaf (it should come out easily, but if it sticks anywhere, just release it from the pan by running the flat side of a knife all around the edge) and turn it upside down to check that the bottom is golden; also, if you knock on it with your knuckles, you should hear a hollow sound. If the bread doesn't seem quite done, return the loaves to the oven to bake for another 5 minutes (there's no need to put the loaves back in their pans—just set them on the oven rack).

Yeast ■ *Breads*

When the loaves are done, turn them out onto racks. Let the bread cool thoroughly before slicing.

To store bread: Wrap each loaf tightly in plastic wrap and keep in a cool place or in the refrigerator; the bread will stay fresh for several days. For longer storage, wrap the loaves in plastic and freeze.

Cleaning Up

If you wash your cups and bowls and measuring spoons as you go along, you will find it much easier to get them clean. It is better to use cold water to remove the sticky bread dough that seems to cling to everything—including your hands—so have a big basin or sink full of cold water at hand and dump your utensils into it as soon as you're finished with them. A plastic mesh scrub ball is helpful in dislodging all the sticky bits. Then rinse your cleaned utensils in warm water.

For the loaf pans, baking sheets, and muffin pans that your doughs have baked in, hot soapy water and a scrub pad do the job best. And, again, the sooner you clean them up, the easier it will be to get them clean.

French Bread

Makes three 12- to 14-inch-long loaves

*I*n France a loaf of crusty bread is essential to every meal. It is bought fresh every day from the *boulangerie,* the bakery, of which there are several in every small village. French children tote the long loaves home under their arms or sometimes balanced on the handlebars of a bicycle.

It's not hard to make this chewy, deliciously crackly loaf, though it takes a little time. The reason the dough is rolled into a long, thin shape is to expose as much of the surface as possible to the high heat and steam of the oven, which creates the glorious golden-brown crust.

1   package (1 scant tablespoon) active dry yeast
1¾   cups warm water
2   teaspoons salt
3   tablespoons whole wheat flour, preferably stone-ground
3½ - 4 cups white flour
Cornmeal

Put the yeast in a large bowl and pour ½ cup of the warm water over it. After a minute stir with your finger to make sure the yeast has dissolved.

Mix the salt with the remaining 1¼ cups water and stir into the dissolved yeast. Put in the whole wheat flour and then add the white flour, a cup at a time, stirring with a big wooden spoon until it becomes difficult to stir. Then scrape the dough out onto a floured work surface, and let it rest while you clean out your bowl.

Scrape up the dough and slap it around, flouring your hands and the work surface as necessary. Then knead until the dough is smooth and elastic—about 10 minutes.

Return the dough to the cleaned, ungreased bowl, cover it with plastic wrap, and let the dough rise in a not-too-warm spot until almost tripled in size—about 2 to 2½ hours.

Punch the dough down and let it rise again, covered, until doubled in size—about 1½ hours.

Scrape the risen dough out onto a floured surface. Divide it into three equal pieces, covering two of them while you form the first loaf this way:

Pat the dough into an oval about 5 or 6 inches long. Fold in half lengthwise and pinch the ends together. Flour your surface again and roll the dough out as if you were mak-ing a clay snake, starting with your two floured hands in the center and moving them outward as you roll to a length of almost 14 inches. Don't press down too hard; roll lightly.

(continued on page 30)

𝒴east ■ ℬreads

Place the loaf on a baking sheet sprinkled with cornmeal, leaving room for the two others. Or place the loaves in lightly buttered or oiled French Bread pans if you have them.

Repeat the process with the other two pieces of dough. Cover them all lightly with a kitchen towel and let rise for 45 minutes.

After the bread has risen for 30 minutes, preheat the oven to 450 degrees. (If you have a baking stone or tiles [see page 65], put them on the oven rack and let them get hot as the oven preheats. Then slide your loaves one by one directly onto this hot oven "floor.") Put a large kettle of water on the stove to boil. Set a shallow pan on the oven floor near the door and close the door.

Yeast ■ *Breads*

When the water boils, quickly open the oven and fill the pan half full of boiling water. Now, using pot holders or mitts to protect your hands, very carefully push the pan onto the oven floor and shut the door to trap the steam inside.

When the loaves are ready to bake—they should look swollen and almost twice their original size—make three shallow diagonal slashes across the top of each, using a sharp knife. Brush or spray the loaves with cold water and quickly slip the baking sheet into the oven, so you lose as little steam as possible.

After 20 minutes, check to see if the bread is a deep golden color; if not, let it bake another few minutes.

Turn off the heat and let the loaves sit 2 or 3 minutes with the door open. To cool, remove the loaves from the oven and prop them up so air can circulate underneath—and listen for the mysterious sound the bread makes as it settles down.

Sourdough Starter

Makes about 5 cups starter

*P*eople love sourdough bread for its pungent, earthy taste. The sourdough starter—usually a mixture of just flour and water that is left to ferment—acts the way yeast does in providing the leavening for a bread dough. The starter has to be coddled—fed frequently and kept warm and protected. In the old days frontiersmen often slept with a jar of sourdough starter to keep it from freezing, for without it they would have had no way to make bread in the wilds of places like the Klondike. That was, of course, before we had reliable dehydrated yeast available.

This recipe creates a starter using our convenient active dry yeast rather than wild or natural yeasts, which are tricky to capture and develop. The mixture of yeast, water, and flour is left to ferment so that it will impart that special sourdough flavor to breads that are made with it.

1 package (1 scant tablespoon) active dry yeast
3 cups warm water
2½ cups white flour

Let the yeast dissolve in ½ cup of the warm water in a large pottery or glass bowl. Stir in the flour and the remaining 2½ cups warm water and mix well. Let stand, covered, in a warm place (such as an oven with a pilot light or on top of a radiator or in a sunny spot) for 24 hours. The mixture will bubble up and froth, then subside.

Pour the mixture into a plastic, glass, or pottery container with a top. Cover it and let it stand in the same warm place for 3 to 5 days.

The starter is now ready to use. Stir it gently with a fork, for it will have separated, and measure out what you need. If you're not using it immediately, keep it in the refrigerator, but be sure to feed it once a week with ½ cup flour and the same amount of warm water. Shake the container to mix. Let it stand in the kitchen overnight, then return it to the refrigerator.

San Francisco Sourdough Bread

Makes one large round loaf

1 package (1 scant tablespoon)
  active dry yeast
½ cup warm water
2 cups Sourdough Starter
  (see previous recipe),
  at room temperature
2 teaspoons salt
3½ - 4 cups white flour
Cornmeal

*T*his makes a round, crusty sourdough loaf.

Dissolve the yeast in the warm water in a large bowl. Then mix in the Sourdough Starter, the salt, and about 3 cups of the white flour, a cup at a time, until the dough becomes hard to stir. Turn the dough out onto a floured work surface and let it rest while you clean the bowl.

Scrape up the dough, slap it around a few times, and then knead it, adding more flour as necessary, until it is smooth and elastic—about 10 minutes. Return the dough to the cleaned bowl, cover with plastic wrap, and let rise until tripled in size—2 to 2½ hours.

Turn the dough out onto a floured surface and form into a large round loaf by molding it with your hands, stretching the dough and tucking it under and then pinching together the seams on the bottom to close them. Sprinkle cornmeal over the center of a baking sheet. Place the loaf on top, cover with a kitchen towel, and let rise until doubled—about 1 hour.

After the dough has risen for 45 minutes, preheat the oven to 450 degrees. Take a sharp knife and make six slashes going one way and then the other in a tic-tac-toe pattern across the top of the loaf.

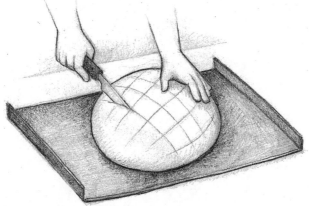

Brush the top and sides of the loaf with water. Bake in the preheated oven for 15 minutes, then reduce the heat to 350 degrees and bake for 25 minutes more, or until the loaf is lightly browned and crusty. Cool on a rack.

Yeast ∎ Breads

Cheese Bread

Makes one 8-inch loaf and one long French loaf

*T*his chewy cheese bread can be baked either in a standard loaf pan or as a long French loaf to be served warm for dinner. Both are so good that we suggest you make one of each, saving the pan loaf for sandwiches.

1 package (1 scant tablespoon) active dry yeast
1¾ cups warm water
2 teaspoons salt
3½ - 4½ cups white flour
1 cup grated sharp cheddar cheese
Cornmeal

Put the yeast in a large bowl and pour ½ cup of the warm water over it. After a minute stir with your finger to make sure the yeast is dissolved.

Mix the remaining 1¼ cups water with the salt and pour it over the dissolved yeast. Stir in the flour, a cup at a time, and when the dough becomes hard to stir, turn it out onto a floured work surface. Let the dough rest while you clean out the bowl.

Scrape up the dough and knead it for 10 minutes, adding more white flour as necessary, until it is smooth and elastic.

Rub the cleaned bowl lightly with soft butter or vegetable oil and return the dough to it, turning to coat. Cover with plastic wrap and let rise until almost tripled in size—2 to 3 hours.

Punch the risen dough down and turn it out onto the floured surface. Spread it out and sprinkle the cheese all over. Then roll the dough up and knead it just long enough to incorporate the cheese into the dough.

Grease an 8-inch loaf pan. Using about two-thirds of the dough, form a loaf as illustrated on page 25 and place it in the greased pan. Roll the remaining dough into a 10-to-12-inch loaf, as directed on page 29, and place on a baking sheet sprinkled with cornmeal. Cover each loaf with a kitchen towel and let rise until doubled in size—about 45 minutes.

After the bread has risen for 30 minutes, preheat the oven to 450 degrees.

Place the loaves in the oven. Remove the French loaf after 18 to 20 minutes, when the top is golden. Turn down the heat to 350 degrees and let the pan loaf bake for another 10 minutes. Cool on racks.

Pear Bread

**Makes two large doughnut-shaped loaves
or two 8-inch pan loaves**

$\mathcal{M}$ake this special bread when fresh pears are really ripe. At our house we often hide the fruit in a dark place for a few days so it will be soft enough for pureeing.

2 medium-sized ripe pears
¼ teaspoon ground ginger
1 package (1 scant tablespoon)
   active dry yeast
⅓ cup warm water
2 tablespoons honey
1½ teaspoons salt
2 large eggs
3½ - 4 cups white flour
GLAZE
1 egg beaten with 1 teaspoon
   water

Peel the pears and remove the cores, as illustrated for apples on page 105. Cut in chunks and put in a blender or food processor. Blend until thoroughly pureed. Add the ginger.

Put the yeast in a large mixing bowl and pour the warm water over it. After a minute stir with your finger to make sure the yeast has dissolved. Add the fruit puree, honey, salt, and eggs, and beat thoroughly. Add 2 cups of the flour and beat with a wooden spoon for about 1 minute. Stir in enough of the remaining flour to make the mixture stiff and hard to mix.

Turn the dough out on a floured work surface and knead for 5 minutes, adding more flour as necessary, until the dough is shiny and smooth. (continued on page 40)

$\mathcal{Y}$east ■ $\mathcal{B}$reads

How to Handle an Egg

Always approach an egg gently. It can easily crack if it is treated roughly. When you do want to crack an egg open, tap it gently but firmly against the side of a bowl and then with your thumbs ease it open over the bowl so that the whole egg drops into it.

If a piece of shell falls into the egg, you will have to fish it out. The best way to do that is to take an empty half shell and use it to scoop up the shell fragment, which is otherwise very hard to catch.

When a recipe calls for just the egg yolk (the yellow center) or the egg white (the more slimy liquid part, which isn't really white until it is cooked), you will have to separate the yolk from the white. The simplest technique is to break the egg very gently and let it fall into your cupped hand that you are holding over a bowl with the fingers very slightly apart. The egg white will fall through your fingers and the yolk will remain in the palm of your hand. Be sure your hands are clean before you start.

Yeast ■ *Breads*

Clean out the bowl, rub the inside with a little soft butter or vegetable oil, and return the dough to it. Let the dough rise, covered with plastic wrap, until doubled in size—about 1½ hours.

Punch the dough down, turn it out on a lightly floured work surface, and divide in half.

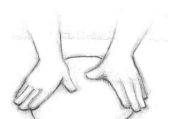

If you want to make the large doughnut shapes, pat each half into a round of about 7 inches. Flour the thumb and the first two fingers of one hand, hold them together at the tips, and plunge them into the center of each round of dough to make a cone-shaped hole, then twirl them around to enlarge the hole to about 3 inches. Grease the outside of an empty small can or cookie cutter and place it in the hole—

otherwise it will close up when baking, and instead of a hole you'll have something that looks like a navel (which is also a nice shape if you want it that way).

Grease a baking sheet, place the doughnuts on it, and cover lightly with a towel. (If you want to make standard pan loaves instead, simply form the dough into two oblongs and place in greased 8-inch loaf pans.) Let rise until doubled in size—about 45 minutes.

After the bread has risen for 30 minutes, preheat the oven to 450 degrees.

Paint the tops of the loaves with the egg glaze and bake in the middle of the preheated oven for 40 minutes. Cool on racks.

Whole Wheat Bread

Makes two 8-inch loaves

*T*his wholesome bread makes good sandwiches. If you live in maple syrup country and can get the dark syrup that isn't grade A, use it as a sweetener instead of honey or molasses.

1½ packages (1½ scant tablespoons) active dry yeast

½ cup warm water

2 cups milk

4 tablespoons (½ stick) butter

½ cup honey, molasses, or brown
sugar, or a combination

2 teaspoons salt

3 cups whole wheat flour,
preferably stone-ground

½ cup wheat germ

2 - 3 cups white flour

Put the yeast in a large bowl and pour the warm water over it. After a minute stir with your finger to make sure the yeast is dissolved.

In a medium saucepan, heat 1 cup of the milk and dissolve the butter, honey or other sweetener, and salt in it. Turn off the heat and stir in the remaining cup of milk.

When the milk mixture is lukewarm (test with your finger), add it to the yeast. Stir in the whole wheat flour, the wheat germ, and about 2 cups of the white flour until the mixture becomes hard to stir. Turn the dough out onto a floured surface and clean out the bowl.

Scrape the dough up and then knead it, adding more white flour as necessary, until it is smooth and elastic—about 10 minutes.

Yeast ■ *Breads*

Rub the inside of the cleaned bowl lightly with soft butter or vegetable oil, and return the dough to it. Leave it to rise, covered with plastic wrap, until doubled in size—about 1½ hours.

Punch the risen dough down, turn it out on the lightly floured surface, and knead it a few turns, then shape it into two loaves, as illustrated on page 25. Grease two 8-inch loaf pans, place the loaves inside them, seam side down, and cover with a kitchen towel. Let rise about 45 minutes, until the dough swells just over the tops of the pans. (continued on page 44)

What's in a Kernel of Wheat?

As the drawing here shows, a kernel of wheat is made up of parts that include bran, which is the outer layer, the interior, called the endosperm, and the wheat germ, which is the richest part. Whole wheat flour contains all of the wheat kernel, and it is often still ground today the way our forefathers did it—by means of two millstones grinding the kernels and spreading the wheat germ evenly throughout. Sometimes the turning of the stones was powered by rushing water, sometimes by the wind. It is possible to get stone-ground whole wheat flour today in health food stores and often in supermarkets. You will notice the wheaty flavor and the more chewy texture of breads made from good whole wheat flour.

bran

endosperm

germ

Yeast ■ Breads

After the loaves have risen for 30 minutes, preheat the oven to 425 degrees. When they are ready, bake for 10 minutes, then lower the heat to 350 degrees and bake for 25 minutes longer, until lightly browned on top. Remove the loaves and cool on racks.

Oatmeal Bread

Makes two cottage loaves or two 9-inch loaves

We like to make this bread in the traditional English form called a cottage loaf—a sort of "double decker" made up of a small round loaf on top of a larger round loaf. Some cooks think the shape originated when ovens were too narrow to accommodate two large loaves side by side. But you can use the same recipe to make two large pan loaves instead.

Put the oats in a large mixing bowl and carefully pour the boiling water over them. Stir in the butter or shortening, dry milk, molasses or syrup, and salt. Let stand until cool. Be sure the oatmeal is really cool—the only way to tell is to stir up the mixture, then slowly stick in a finger and make sure you can hold it there comfortably.

Dissolve the yeast in the warm water. Add this to the oatmeal mixture. Stir in the whole wheat flour and about 2 cups of the white flour until the dough becomes difficult to stir.

Turn the dough out onto a floured work surface and let it rest

2	cups rolled oats
3	cups boiling water
4	tablespoons (½ stick) butter or
	¼ cup vegetable shortening
¼	cup nonfat dry milk
¼	cup molasses or maple syrup
2	teaspoons salt
2	packages (2 scant tablespoons)
	active dry yeast
½	cup warm water
2	cups whole wheat flour
2½ - 3½	cups white flour
⅔	cup raisins

while you clean out your bowl. Then start kneading, adding more white flour as necessary. It will be a very sticky dough, and you'll have to keep adding more flour in order to knead—about 10 minutes of kneading and 1 additional cup of white flour should be enough. Sprinkle the raisins over the dough and knead a little longer to work them in evenly.

Rub the inside of the cleaned bowl lightly with soft butter or vegetable shortening and place the dough in it, turning to coat. Let rise, covered with plastic wrap, until doubled in size—about 1½ hours.

Turn the dough out and divide it in half.* To make cottage loaves, divide each half into two pieces of different size—the piece for the topknot should be one-third the size of the bottom. Separate all these pieces and cover with a kitchen towel, letting them simply sit on your work area for 45 minutes.

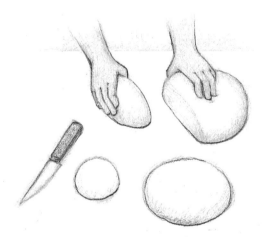

Note: If you want to make regular loaves, simply form the dough into the usual loaf shapes and place in two greased 9-inch standard loaf pans. Cover and let rise for 45 minutes, then bake in a preheated 375-degree oven for 45 minutes.

Yeast ■ Breads

Now take the larger pieces and pat each out into a flat 7-inch circle. With a sharp knife, make a cross about 1 inch deep and 1½ inches across in the middle of each circle.

Shape the smaller pieces into balls and settle them into the openings made by the crosses. Now, with the thumb and first two fingers of one hand, press a hole through the center of each ball of dough, push-

ing straight down to the bottom of the dough. Thoroughly grease a large baking sheet. With a spatula, transfer the loaves to the baking sheet, setting them far apart. Let rest 10 minutes.

Place the baking sheet on the lowest shelf of an unlit oven and set the temperature at 450 degrees. As the oven heats up, the loaves will expand, which is fun to watch if your oven has a glass door and a light inside. After 15 minutes, reduce the temperature to 375 degrees and bake for another 25 minutes. Then remove the loaves and cool on racks.

Seeded Bread

Makes two 8-inch loaves

*T*his bread has a wonderful nutty flavor and makes great sandwiches, particularly with peanut butter or cream cheese. It is also delicious toasted for breakfast and spread with butter and honey. Nourishing, too.

1½ packages (1½ scant tablespoons) active dry yeast
3 cups warm water
3 tablespoons honey or maple syrup
¼ cup vegetable or peanut oil
2 teaspoons salt
½ cup bran
3 cups whole wheat flour
3 - 3½ cups white flour
2 tablespoons poppy seeds
3 tablespoons sesame seeds
¼ cup pumpkin seeds

Put the yeast in a large bowl and pour ¼ cup of the warm water over it. After a minute stir with your finger to make sure the yeast has dissolved.

Add the remaining 2¾ cups water, the honey or syrup, oil, salt, bran, whole wheat flour, and about 2 cups of the white flour and stir, adding flour until the dough becomes difficult to stir.

Turn the dough out onto a floured work surface, spread it out, and sprinkle the three kinds of seeds on top. Knead the dough for about 10 minutes, adding more flour as necessary until the dough is smooth and bouncy, although it will be a little sticky.

Clean out your bowl and oil it lightly. Return the dough to it, cover with plastic wrap, and leave to rise until doubled in size— about 1¼ hours.

Turn the dough out onto a lightly floured work surface, knead it a couple of turns, and divide it in half. Form each half into an 8-inch loaf, as illustrated on page 25. Grease two 8-inch loaf pans. Place the loaves in the pans, seam side down, cover with a kitchen towel, and let rise just above the tops of the pans—about 40 minutes.

After the loaves have risen for 25 minutes, preheat the oven to 350 degrees.

Bake in the preheated oven for 45 minutes. Remove the pans and turn the loaves out onto racks to let cool before slicing.

Scandinavian Rye Bread

Makes three medium-sized round loaves

$\mathcal{T}$his recipe makes dark, round, shiny loaves that smell deliciously of orange and spices. It's quite a bit of work to grate the skins of six oranges, but not if you divide it up among friends. Thick slices of this bread go well with a soup or salad or scrambled eggs and make a complete supper. It's nice to have some soft, mild cheese with the bread, too.

2   tablespoons fennel seeds
2   tablespoons caraway seeds
1   cup water
½   cup unsulfured molasses
Grated rind of 6 oranges
     (see box)
1   tablespoon butter
2   teaspoons salt
2   cups buttermilk
½   teaspoon baking soda
2   packages (2 scant tablespoons)
     active dry yeast
¼   cup warm water
4   cups rye flour
4   cups white flour
GLAZE
1   tablespoon molasses mixed
     with 1 tablespoon water

Put the fennel and caraway seeds between sheets of paper and pound gently with a rolling pin to crush them.

Put the water, molasses, grated orange rind, crushed fennel and caraway seeds, butter, and salt in a medium saucepan. Heat slowly until the butter melts. Turn off the heat, add the buttermilk and baking soda, and stir. Set aside to cool to lukewarm (test with your finger).

Grating Oranges and Lemons

If you have a four-sided grater, use the large side with the smaller holes. Rub an orange or lemon against the rough-edged holes until the rind is grated through the holes, then turn the orange or lemon and grate the rind in another area. Continue to do this all around the fruit until you are down to the white pith. Don't grate that—it will be bitter. What you will have in the center of the grater is a mound of finely grated bright orange or bright yellow rind called the zest. Scrape every bit of it off the grater so you collect it all.

Dissolve the yeast in the ¼ cup warm water in a large mixing bowl.

Stir the cooled molasses-buttermilk mixture into the yeast. Add the rye flour, then 2½ cups of the white, a cup or so at a time, stirring thoroughly to mix.

Turn the dough out onto a floured work surface and let it rest while you clean out the bowl.

Sprinkle white flour on top of the dough and on your hands,

and knead. This dough will be sticky, and you'll have to keep flouring often. Knead for 10 minutes. You may find it hard going, so take turns with a friend. When you have used up the remaining white flour, the dough will be smooth and alive-feeling, even though it may still be just a little sticky in the middle.

Rub the inside of the cleaned bowl lightly with soft butter or vegetable oil and return the dough to it, turning to coat. Cover with plastic wrap and let rise until doubled in size—about 1½ hours.

Punch down the risen dough. Turn it out on the floured surface and knead it a couple of turns. Divide into three equal parts and shape each third into a round loaf, molding the sides down and under and pinching the seams together at the bottom.

Grease a large baking sheet and place the loaves on it far apart. Let them rise under a kitchen towel for about 1 hour, or until doubled in size.

After the loaves have risen for 45 minutes, preheat the oven to 375 degrees.

Just before baking, cut a large cross about ⅓ inch deep in the center of each loaf, using a sharp knife dipped in flour.

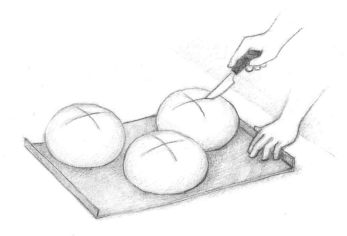

Bake the loaves in the preheated oven for 35 minutes. Using pot holders, pull out the baking sheets long enough to brush the loaves with the glaze. Return to the oven and bake for 5 minutes longer. Remove to racks and cool.

Pumpernickel Bread

Makes two large round loaves

*L*ots of stories have been told to explain the word "pumpernickel"—a tale about Napoleon says he rejected the dark bread he was given in Prussia and gave it to his horse. *"Pain pour Nicole,"* he said: "Bread for my horse." Knowing how dependent he was on Nicole, he sacrificed the hearty loaf he might have enjoyed himself.

1 package (1 scant tablespoon)
     active dry yeast
1 cup warm water
1 tablespoon carob powder
     or unsweetened cocoa
1 cup Sourdough Starter
     (page 32), at room
     temperature
1½ cups plain yogurt,
     at room temperature
4 teaspoons salt
¼ cup vegetable shortening,
     melted
1 cup bran
2 cups rye flour
2 cups whole wheat flour
2 - 2½ cups white flour

Put the yeast in a large bowl and pour the warm water over it.

Add the carob powder or cocoa to the yeast and stir with your finger to dissolve thoroughly, then add the Sourdough Starter, yogurt, salt, and shortening (be sure it is not too hot—just warm). Mix well.

Stir in the bran, the rye and whole wheat flours, and almost 2 cups of the white flour until the dough gets too hard to stir. Then turn it out on a floured work surface and let it rest while you clean out the bowl.

Scrape up the dough and

start to knead, adding more white flour as necessary. This will be a sticky dough and will absorb flour as you knead. Ten minutes will be enough, even if it is still a little sticky.

Rub the inside of the cleaned bowl lightly with vegetable shortening and return the dough to it, turning to coat. Cover with plastic wrap and let rise until doubled in size—about 2 hours.

Punch the risen dough down and turn it out onto the floured surface. Divide in half. Shape each half into a large round, molding the sides down and under and pinching the seams together at the bottom.

Grease a large baking sheet and place the loaves far apart on it. Cover loosely with a kitchen towel and let rise until doubled in size—about 45 minutes.

After the loaves have risen for 30 minutes, preheat the oven to 350 degrees.

Paint the tops of the loaves all over with the egg glaze,

GLAZE
1 egg beaten with
   1 teaspoon water
TOPPING
About ½ cup cracked wheat
   or wheat germ

then sprinkle either cracked wheat or wheat germ generously over the surface. Bake in the preheated oven for 1 hour. Remove to racks and let cool.

Focaccia

Makes one oval loaf

*F*ocaccia (*foe-catch-eeya*), which means "hearth," is a flattish Italian bread baked on the hearth, topped with herbs, cheese, peppers, olives, even meats, so that a good helping of it would be satisfying enough for a midday meal. No doubt the Italian housewife on baking day would pull off a hunk of dough, season it with whatever she had on hand for toppings, and without even waiting for it to rise again, slip the dough onto the oven floor, which was heated up to bake the weekly supply of bread for her family. When we were trying some focaccias in our kitchen, one of the teenage bakers suggested a sweet topping of sugar and cinnamon. So we tried it, and it made a delicious breakfast bread.

1 package (1 scant tablespoon) active dry yeast

1¼ cups warm water

1 teaspoon salt

2¼ - 2½ cups all-purpose flour

2 teaspoons olive oil or vegetable oil

Cornmeal

TOPPINGS (pages 58 and 60)

Put the yeast in a large mixing bowl and pour ¼ cup of the warm water over it. Let stand for a few minutes to dissolve the yeast, then with your finger smear the yeast around to make sure it is softened. Mix the salt with the rest of the water, and pour it into the bowl along with 2¼ cups of flour. Continue to stir vigorously until well mixed, although this dough will be quite sticky.

Lightly flour your work surface and scrape the dough out of the bowl onto it. Now start kneading gently with floured hands, not pushing the dough heavily against the counter but with a light touch pushing it away from you and scooping it up again with the help of a dough scraper or a spatula. Continue to knead gently for about 2 minutes, adding a little more flour to your hands and to the work surface as needed to keep the dough from sticking.

Wash out your mixing bowl, dry it, and oil it lightly, using about ½ teaspoon of the olive oil. Put the dough in the bowl and turn it around to grease it all over. Cover the bowl tightly with plastic wrap, and leave the dough to rise until it has more than doubled in size. It should take about an hour, depending on how warm the kitchen is.

Generously sprinkle cornmeal over an 8-by-11-inch area of a baking sheet. Turn the dough out onto a floured work surface and start patting it into an oval shape. It will be sticky and resistant, so when you have it partially shaped, distribute the remaining 1½ teaspoons olive oil over the top, spreading the oil with your fingers, and transfer the dough to the prepared baking sheet. Now continue to stretch and shape the dough with your oiled fingers until it is about 8 by 11 inches.

Use one of the three suggested savory toppings to flavor and decorate the focaccia, or if you like a sweet bread for breakfast or tea, try topping 4.

Preheat the oven to 425 degrees. After you have spread the dough with one of the toppings, let it rest and rise slightly for 15 minutes.

Bake the focaccia in the preheated oven for 25 minutes. Remove and serve warm.

Filled Breads ■ Flatbreads

■ Topping 1 ■

1½   teaspoons kosher or coarse sea salt

1   large garlic clove, peeled (see box)

1   large sprig fresh rosemary or 1 tablespoon dried

Sprinkle the salt over the shaped dough. Cut the garlic clove into very thin slices, then cut the larger pieces in half horizontally. Now insert slices of the garlic at intervals all over the top of the dough, embedding them deeply and pinching pieces of dough over the top so the garlic is covered. Top each garlic insertion with several of the thin leaves of rosemary.

■ Topping 2 ■

1   teaspoon kosher or coarse sea salt

8   sun-dried tomatoes, soaked for 10-15 minutes
    in hot water to cover

1   cup coarsely grated flavorful cheese, such as Gouda,
    cheddar, or Swiss

Sprinkle the salt over the shaped dough. Drain the tomatoes and pat them dry. Cut into halves and distribute them at intervals over the dough. Sprinkle on the grated cheese, covering the entire surface.

How to Handle Garlic

First, to break up a whole head of garlic so you can extract one or two cloves, set it on a cutting board, stem side up, and place the flat side of a big knife on top or, if that makes your parents nervous, use a spatula

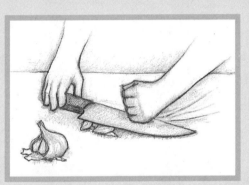

instead. Now make a fist and wham it against the side of the knife or spatula once or twice until the head breaks apart and the cloves scatter.

To peel a clove, place the flat side of your big knife or spatula on top of the clove and again wham it firmly with your fist. You'll find that the force of the punch will have made the inside of the clove burst through the skin so that the skin is shattered and can now be easily removed with your fingers.

At this point slice the garlic clove with a small knife.

■ Topping 3 ■

1   medium onion, peeled and sliced thin (see box)
½   large red pepper, seeds removed, cut in ¼-inch slices
2   teaspoons olive oil
1   teaspoon kosher or coarse sea salt
8-10   black kalamata olives, pits removed, cut in half

Sauté the onion and red pepper in the olive oil in a medium pan, starting over medium-high heat and reducing to low after 1 minute. When the vegetables have softened—about 5 minutes—remove from the heat and let cool. Sprinkle the salt over the shaped dough, then spread the onion and pepper on top and distribute olive halves at intervals, tucking them down into the vegetables.

■ Topping 4 ■

1   tablespoon butter, at room temperature
¼   cup sugar
1   teaspoon ground cinnamon

If you are making this sweet topping, do not spread olive oil on the dough. Instead, smear the softened butter all over the top. Mix the sugar and cinnamon together and sprinkle that evenly over the surface.

Peeling and Slicing Onions

First, cut your onion in half with a large knife, holding the onion with the thumb and forefinger of one hand and with the other hand slicing down from the stem end to the root. Peel off all the papery outside skin. Now lay one side of the onion, cut side down, on a chopping board. Hold the onion half with one hand with your fingers tucked under, and, starting at the

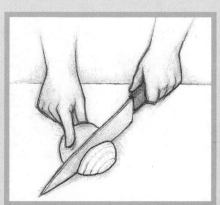

stem end, cut even-sized slices with the knife, moving your other hand back after each slice, with the fingers always tucked under until you get to the root end. Discard the root piece.

Pizza

Makes two 13-inch pizzas

DOUGH

1 package (1 scant tablespoon)
   active dry yeast
1½ cups warm water
2 teaspoons salt
3⅓ cups white flour
2 tablespoons olive oil
Cornmeal

FILLING SUGGESTIONS

for two 13-inch pizzas

6 cups canned plum tomatoes,
   drained and chopped
2 teaspoons dried oregano
   or basil
About 16 strips anchovy fillets or
   ham or Italian salami
1 cup black olives, pitted
   and halved
2 cups diced mozzarella cheese
¼ cup grated Parmesan cheese
1-2 tablespoons olive oil

*I*f you want to make pizza like the experts, you'll need tiles or a baking stone to put onto the rack of the oven (see page 65) and a baker's paddle to slip the formed and filled pizza down onto the hot tiles or stone. That's certainly the way to get a pizza that is really crusty on the bottom. But if all this extra equipment and tricky technique is too much for you, you can simply form and bake your pizza on a large baking sheet and you'll still have a glorious homemade pizza—better than store-bought.

Put the yeast in a large bowl and pour ½ cup of the water over it. After a minute stir with your finger to make sure the yeast is dissolved.

Stir the salt into the remaining 1 cup water, then pour the

mixture over the dissolved yeast, along with 3 cups of the flour and the olive oil. Stir well to mix.

Turn the dough out onto a floured work surface and let it rest while you clean the bowl.

Knead the dough, adding more flour as necessary, until it is smooth, elastic, and no longer sticky—about 10 minutes.

Oil the cleaned bowl lightly and return the dough to it, turning to coat. Cover the bowl with plastic wrap and let the dough rise until doubled in size—about 1½ hours.

Fifteen minutes before the rising time is up, set the tiles or baking stone, if you are using one, in place on the middle rack of the oven. Preheat the oven to 450 degrees.

Assemble all the filling ingredients that you plan to use.

Punch down the risen dough and turn it out onto a large, well-floured work surface.

Divide the dough in half. Cover one of the halves with a kitchen towel while you work with the other one.

Pat the dough into a circle. Using a floured rolling pin, roll the dough out from the center toward the edges, picking it up and turning it between rollings. It will be bouncy and resistant, so when you've increased the circle as much as you can by rolling, pick up the dough and, using both fists, twirl it around to enlarge the circle even further, as you've seen the experts do in pizza parlor windows. The important thing is to get the dough as thin and even as possible.

Filled Breads ■ Flatbreads

When you have a circle about 13 inches in diameter, transfer it to a paddle (if you're using tiles or a baking stone) or to a baking sheet, either of which you've sprinkled liberally with cornmeal. Pat the edges of the dough to even out your circle. Now arrange the filling on the pizza dough as follows, leaving a ½-inch border.

Spread half of the well-drained tomatoes over the pizza dough. Sprinkle on half the oregano or basil and distribute half the olives around evenly. Arrange half the anchovies or meats, sprinkle on half the amount of the two cheeses, and drizzle olive oil over the surface. (*continued on page 66*)

Baking Stones and Tiles

In the old days breads were often baked in brick or clay ovens directly on the oven floor. As a result, they developed a wonderful crust that is hard to achieve in our modern gas or electric ovens. To try to reproduce the effect of that hot brick or clay oven floor, home bakers today often use tiles laid on the oven rack or a large baking stone, which you can get at specialty stores. The baking stone or tiles have already been placed in the oven when you preheat it, so by the time you slide your loaves in, the "floor" is nice and hot. Certain breads—such as French loaves, pizzas, focaccias, calzones, and pitas—are particularly good baked this way.

If you buy tiles or a stone, you might also want to get yourself a baker's paddle (called a peel) with a long handle. The unbaked bread goes directly on the paddle, which has been sprinkled with cornmeal so the dough won't stick, and then you plunge the paddle into the hot oven, jerk the handle, and pull it away quickly, leaving the bread—hopefully—on the oven floor.

Another old-fashioned baking device is a stone—usually soapstone—that is placed on top of the stove burner. The advantage here is that the baking stone gives you a very even heat, and you don't even need to grease the stone because the dough doesn't stick to it. It's particularly useful for baking pancakes and scones and naans.

Your oven should be piping hot now. To transfer the filled pizza to the hot surface of the tiles or baking stone (if you are using one of them) is quite a trick. Place the paddle a couple of inches above the hot surface, then jerk it suddenly in a quick, sure motion toward you, letting the pizza slip off the paddle onto the tiles or stone. If it doesn't work the first time, try again after loosening the pizza all around with a spatula. Of course, if you are using the baking sheet, just place that in the oven.

Bake for about 12 minutes (in the meantime, prepare your second pizza so it will be ready to go into the oven as soon as the first one is done).* Then look to see if the edges of the dough have puffed and browned lightly. If so, the pizza is done; if not, bake a few minutes more. Remove and serve bubbling hot.

Note: If you want to make only one pizza, you can refrigerate or freeze half the dough, securely wrapped in plastic wrap. You will need only half the amount of filling.

Filled Breads ■ Flatbreads

Calzone

**Makes three calzones about 8 inches long,
to serve 4 to 6**

$\mathcal{T}$he word *calzone* means "pants leg" in Italian, and by a stretch of the imagination this filled bread resembles a baggy trouser leg when it comes out of the oven. The bread can be filled with almost anything that strikes your fancy—simply follow generally the same proportions as those listed under "Filling" in the ingredients list. Be sure that the seasonings are assertive and that you include some cheese, so that when you cut through the warm crust you will have a flow of warm cheese and a heady scent of garlic and herbs.

1½ teaspoons (½ package) active dry yeast
1 cup warm water
2 tablespoons olive oil
1 teaspoon salt
¼ cup cake flour (not the self-rising kind)
About 2 cups white flour, preferably unbleached
FILLING (page 68)

Put the yeast in a medium bowl and pour ¼ cup of the warm water over it. Stir with your finger to make sure the granules have dissolved. Add, stirring with a big spoon, the remaining ¾ cup water, the olive oil, salt, cake flour, and as much of the white flour as can be absorbed before the dough gets too stiff.

Turn the dough out on a floured work surface and let it rest while you clean the bowl. Knead the dough for 5 to 6 minutes,

FILLING

4 ounces grated mozzarella
cheese

4 ounces fresh goat cheese or
cream cheese

3 tablespoons grated Swiss
cheese or Parmesan or a
combination

1 large garlic clove, peeled and
minced

½ teaspoon salt

3 tablespoons chopped mixed
fresh herbs, such as Italian
parsley, basil, oregano, chives,
savory

¼ pound salami or prosciutto
(Italian-style ham) or ham,
thinly sliced and chopped

Freshly ground pepper

adding more white flour as necessary, until it is smooth and springy. Return it to the clean bowl, cover with plastic wrap, and let rise until doubled in size—about 1½ hours.

Meanwhile, prepare the filling, mixing all the ingredients together. Divide it into three equal portions.

If you have a baking stone or tiles (see page 65), put them in the oven and preheat to 400 degrees. If you don't have them, use baking sheets and slip them into the oven 5 minutes before you are ready to bake so they will get hot.

Turn the risen dough out onto a floured work surface and divide it into three equal pieces. With a lightly floured rolling pin, roll out one piece to an oval about 8 inches long and 6 inches at its widest. Spoon one portion of the filling down the middle, brush the outside rim of the dough all around with the egg glaze, then pull up the sides and ends of the dough so they meet.

Filled Breads ■ Flatbreads

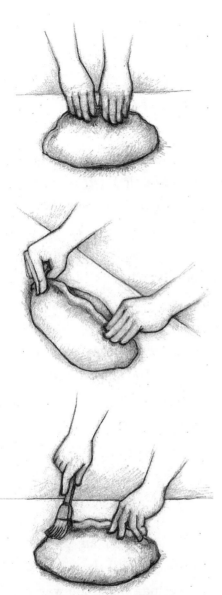

GLAZE

1   egg beaten with 1 teaspoon
    water
Cornmeal

Pinch the sides and ends securely together, and fold the pinched edge over and smooth it down. Now paint the tops and sides with egg glaze, particularly generously around the seams, and press down firmly again so there is no leakage. Repeat the rolling and filling with the two remaining pieces of dough. Put the filled loaves on a paddle or a baking sheet that you have sprinkled thoroughly with cornmeal. Let them rest for 5 minutes.

Slip the calzones onto the hot oven tiles or baking stone or baking sheets by jerking away the paddle or sheet they are on. The calzones should slip off easily, but if they don't, ease them off with the help of a spatula. Bake for 30 minutes. Serve warm.

Pita

Makes twelve 6-inch pitas

*P*itas have become almost as popular in America these days as they are in the Middle East. In many villages there, families do not have their own ovens. So housewives make the dough at home and send the children out, carrying large wooden trays or baskets on their heads, to deliver the rounds to the village baker to be baked. They have to watch carefully to see that their own family's loaves are not lost among others, and sometimes they mark their dough with a stick. To be sure that the pita you are eating is your own, the best way is to bake it yourself. Eat the pitas warm from your own oven, filled with meat, chicken, a salad, or a mixture of scrambled eggs and vegetables.

1   package (1 scant tablespoon)
      active dry yeast
1½ cups warm water
1   tablespoon olive oil
1   teaspoon salt
About 3½ cups white flour

Sprinkle the yeast into a large bowl and pour ½ cup of the warm water on top. Stir with your finger until the yeast is dissolved and no longer grainy. Add the remaining 1 cup water, olive oil, and salt, and mix well. Stir in most of the flour until the dough holds together and becomes hard to stir.

Turn the dough out onto a floured surface. Knead it for about 10 minutes, adding more flour as necessary to make a firm, elastic dough. Wash and dry the bowl thoroughly, rub the inside with additional oil, put the dough in, turning to coat it, and cover the bowl with plastic wrap. Let the dough rise in a warm place until doubled in size—about 1½ hours.

Turn the dough out onto a large, lightly floured surface and roll it with the palms of your hands into a long roll. With a dough scraper or knife, cut the roll into twelve equal sections. Form each section into a ball about the size of a Ping-Pong ball by rolling it around in your hands. After you have formed each ball, set it aside and cover with a towel. Let the balls rest for 5 minutes.

Flour your work surface lightly, and using a heavy rolling pin, roll each ball out to a disk 6 inches in diameter. The dough will resist you, so roll firmly, turning the dough frequently on the floured surface and adding a little more flour as necessary so that it doesn't stick. Repeat with the remaining balls of dough, then cover the circles with a towel and let them rest for 15 minutes.

Meanwhile, preheat the oven to 500 degrees and put in two baking sheets or a baking stone or tiles to heat up.

When the oven is hot, slide the oven rack out just a bit. Working carefully (the pans will be hot) and using a spatula, slide a disk onto one part of the pan or baking stone; you should be able to get three on each pan. Quickly shut the oven door and don't peek for 1 minute; then open the door slightly and you'll see that the rounds of dough have puffed up like balloons (of course, if you have a glass oven door you can watch it all happen).

Continue baking for 2 minutes more, then remove the pitas one by one with a spatula, resting them on a cool surface while you bake the remaining ones. Gradually, they will deflate as they cool, although some may surprise you and stay puffed up. To fill a pita, just break it open and put the filling in the pocket (that is why this bread is sometimes called pocket bread).

To keep pitas, stack them and put them in a plastic bag, squeezing out the air and tightly closing the open end. Store in the refrigerator or freezer. You'll also find they are good when toasted.

Filled Breads ■ Flatbreads

Naan

Makes nine breads

*A*ccording to Madhur Jaffrey, the expert on Indian cooking who has done many television shows introducing the English-speaking world to the wonders of Asian food, the naan (pronounced to rhyme with John) is made in some version from the southern part of Russia to northern India, baked in clay, brick, or stone ovens. Her simplified version bakes the thin rounds of bread first on top of the stove and then under the broiler. Eat them warm. They are good with any kind of spicy food or just with a plain hamburger.

3¾ cups white flour
1 teaspoon baking powder
¼ teaspoon salt
About 1¾ cups plain yogurt
Softened butter

Toss the flour, baking powder, and salt together in a bowl. Slowly stir in as much yogurt as you need until you have a soft dough that holds together.

Turn the dough out onto a lightly floured work surface and knead it for about 10 minutes. Form it into a ball and put it back in the clean bowl, cover it with a dampened towel, and set it aside in a warm place for 1½ hours.

Heat a cast-iron frying pan or a baking stone over low to medium heat. Preheat the broiler. (*continued on page 74*)

Filled Breads ■ Flatbreads

Turn the dough out of the bowl again and knead briefly, about half a minute. Divide the dough into nine equal parts and cover with a towel. Take one portion and roll it into a ball, then flatten it with the heel of your hand. Now, with a rolling pin, roll it out to a circle about ⅛ inch thick and almost 8 inches in diameter.

Test your pan or baking stone by sprinkling a few drops of water on top. If they sizzle, the surface is hot enough. Pick up the round of dough and slap it onto the hot surface. Turn the heat down a little and let the naan cook slowly for 4 minutes or so; it will probably puff up in places.

Now put the whole skillet or baking stone under the broiler for 1 to 1½ minutes, or until the naan is completely puffed up and there are a few reddish-brown spots on top. Remove and brush with a little butter, if you like. Make the rest of the naans in the same way, stacking them up as they are done and covering them with a kitchen towel.

Serve warm.

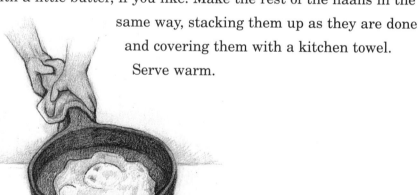

Hoe Cakes

Makes about twelve cakes

*I*n colonial America, the earliest form of corn bread was called an "ash cake" or "hoe cake," for the cooking was done in hot ashes and the handiest tool that would hold the cakes in the heat long enough to cook them was a garden hoe. Nowadays, a method almost as simple, and one that results in better flavor, requires an iron skillet, a little bacon fat or vegetable shortening, and a quick fire. (The cakes can also be done over a campfire.) To add real Yankee flavor, stir in 1 tablespoon of maple syrup when mixing the ingredients.

2 cups cornmeal
1 teaspoon salt
About 2 cups boiling water
1 tablespoon maple syrup (optional)
Bacon fat or vegetable shortening for frying

Mix the cornmeal with the salt in a medium bowl. Carefully add enough boiling water—along with the maple syrup, if you are using it—to make a stiff dough, and stir. Let it stand a few minutes.

Put enough fat in a skillet to cover the bottom, and heat until it is sizzling.

With your hands, shape the dough into 12 small cakes about the size of a little hamburger, and fry them on each side until crusty and brown. Turn once.

Serve very hot—they're wonderful with jelly or butter.

Baked Doughnuts

Makes about two dozen doughnuts
plus two dozen holes

*T*raditionally, doughnuts are cooked by frying the rings of dough in a large pot of boiling hot fat. It can be very treacherous dropping them into the fat and extracting them when they're done—hot fat is apt to splatter and you could get burned. So we devised a method of baking doughnuts in the oven instead of frying them. After they're baked, you paint them with warm butter and roll them in cinnamon sugar—and they are light and delicious, particularly when eaten warm from the oven.

1½ cups milk
⅓ cup vegetable shortening
2 tablespoons sugar
3 tablespoons light brown sugar
2 packages (2 scant tablespoons) active dry yeast
⅓ cup warm water
2 teaspoons salt
2 teaspoons nutmeg (see box, page 91)
2 large eggs
4½ cups white flour, plus about ⅓ cup for dusting

COATING

4 tablespoons (½ stick) butter
¾ cup sugar
1 teaspoon ground cinnamon

Pour the milk into a saucepan and warm it over low heat. When bubbles begin to appear, stir in the shortening and continue stirring until it has melted. Stir in both kinds of sugar and set aside to cool.

Put the yeast in a large bowl and pour the water over it. Let it sit for a minute, then stir with your finger until the yeast is dissolved.

When the milk mixture has cooled (test it by holding your finger in it to make sure), pour it over the dissolved yeast. Stir in the salt and nutmeg. Lightly beat the eggs with a fork, just enough to blend the yolks and whites, and add them along with 2 cups of the flour. Stir vigorously with a big spoon until everything is thoroughly blended. Add another cup of flour and stir again until blended. Add the final 1½ cups and beat until smooth.

Cover the bowl with a kitchen towel and set aside to rise until doubled in size—about 1 hour.

Preheat the oven to 450 degrees. Grease two large baking sheets.

Sprinkle a work surface generously with flour and then scrape the dough out onto it. With a floured rolling pin, roll the dough out into a big circle about ½ inch thick. This is a very soft, moist dough, and you will need a generous amount of flour to keep it from sticking. Dip a 3-inch doughnut cutter into the flour, then sharply press it into the dough and pull the cutter up quickly. Lift out the circle of dough and place it on the baking sheet. Continue cutting out circles and placing them 1 inch apart until you have filled the two baking sheets. *(continued on page 78)*

Breakfast ■ Breads

Let the doughnuts rise for 20 minutes, uncovered.

After filling the two baking sheets, you will still have some leftover dough. Scoop it up, press it into a ball, cover it, and set it aside, along with all the holes that are left from cutting out the rings.

Bake the first batch of doughnuts for 10 minutes, or until the tops are golden brown. Remove all that look done, and if the ones in the center of the baking sheet require a little more browning, return them to the oven for 2 to 3 minutes. Leave the oven on.

Meanwhile, melt the butter in a small pan. Put the sugar and cinnamon together on a large piece of waxed paper and stir them with your fingers until mixed. Brush the baked doughnuts thoroughly with melted butter, then remove them to the waxed paper and turn them in the cinnamon sugar.

Pat the remaining reserved dough into a circle and cut out as many doughnut rings as you can. Arrange them along with the dough holes on one of the baking sheets that you've just used.

Let rise for 20 minutes, then bake 10 minutes, as you did the first batch. Brush with butter and roll in the cinnamon sugar.

The doughnuts are best eaten still warm, but they can be reheated. They can also be frozen and heated up again.

Bagels

Makes eighteen bagels

*B*agels are great fun to make at home, and they taste so good when they have been freshly baked. Surprisingly, unlike most breads or rolls, they are first cooked gently in slightly sugared water before they are put into a hot oven to become crusty as a turtle.

Bagels are particularly popular today, perhaps because they are so chewy and satisfying and are a great carrier of flavors, from cream cheese and smoked salmon to peanut butter and jam. They can be made plain or topped with sesame seeds, poppy seeds, or onions, as suggested in the variations on page 81.

1 package (1 scant tablespoon) active dry yeast
2 - 4 tablespoons sugar
1 cup warm milk, skim or whole
2 tablespoons vegetable oil
1 teaspoon salt
2 large eggs
3¼ - 3¾ cups white flour
1 egg white, lightly beaten (see page 39)

Put the yeast and 1 tablespoon of the sugar in a large bowl, and pour in ¼ cup of the warm milk. Stir with your finger to make sure the yeast and sugar are dissolved, then add 1 more tablespoon of the sugar, the remaining ¾ cup milk, the oil, salt, and eggs, and beat thoroughly. Stir in 3¼ cups of flour and mix until you have a firm dough.

Turn the dough out onto a floured work surface and knead,

adding more flour as necessary, until you have a smooth, bouncy dough—about 5 minutes. Clean out the bowl, oil it lightly, and return the dough to it. Cover with plastic wrap and let rise until doubled in size—about 40 minutes.

Turn the dough out onto a lightly floured work surface and divide it into eighteen equal-sized pieces. Cover them lightly with a towel.

One by one, shape each piece into a round and flatten it into a circle about 2½ inches in diameter. Now make a hole in the center by thrusting in your index finger, which you have dipped first into flour. Twirl  your finger around the hole to enlarge it, then widen it further by gently pulling back the edges of the circle and evening and plumping up the roll as you do so. Place the rolls on a tray and let them rest for 20 minutes.

Meanwhile, oil two baking sheets and preheat the oven to 375 degrees. Fill a large wide pan with boiling water; you can use a big skillet, or even two if you want to make the poaching process go faster. Put 1 tablespoon of sugar in each pan and bring to a boil, then reduce the water to a simmer.

With a spatula, scoop up the first of the circles you shaped and drop it gently into the simmering water. Follow with three others so you have four to a pan. Repeat with the other pan if you are poaching two panfuls at a time. The circles of dough will rise to the sur-

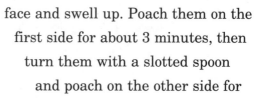

face and swell up. Poach them on the first side for about 3 minutes, then turn them with a slotted spoon and poach on the other side for 3 minutes. If you notice that the holes seem to be closing up, ease them open with the handle of a wooden spoon.

Remove the bagels with a slotted spoon, shaking each one gently to remove the water, and place them slightly apart on the baking sheets. Paint the tops with egg white and bake in the preheated oven for 30 minutes, until lightly browned. Remove the pans from the oven and cool the bagels on racks.

For Sesame Seed Bagels: After you have painted the bagels with egg white, sprinkle about ½ teaspoon sesame seeds over the top of each bagel and bake.

For Poppy Seed Bagels: After you have painted the bagels with egg white, sprinkle about ½ teaspoon poppy seeds over the top of each bagel and bake.

For Onion Bagels: Peel and thinly slice 2 large onions, as described on page 61. Sauté the slices gently in 3 tablespoons butter for 10 minutes. After you have painted the bagels with egg white, distribute the sautéed onion slices equally over the tops and bake.

English Muffins

Makes one dozen muffins

*I*f you and your family like English muffins for breakfast, you'll get a kick out of producing these yummy muffins for about one-sixth the price you would pay for them in the supermarket. But first start saving six-ounce tuna fish or kitty food cans. Before they are thrown out, retrieve them, wash them well, and remove the bottoms with a can opener so that you have just the rings left. When you have four or five, you are ready to make English muffins. These are not rich muffins, because after they have been baked in a skillet, just before serving, they are meant to be split and toasted and slathered with butter and jam or marmalade.

1   package (1 scant tablespoon) active dry yeast
1   tablespoon sugar
1½ cups warm water
3   tablespoons nonfat dry milk
2   teaspoons salt
2¼ - 2¾ cups white flour
¼   teaspoon baking soda

Put the yeast and sugar in a large bowl and pour ½ cup of the warm water over. After a minute stir with your finger to make sure the yeast and sugar are dissolved.

Add the remaining cup of water to the bowl along with the dry milk and salt. Stir with a big wooden spoon until well mixed. Add 2 cups of the flour and stir well, then add about ½ cup more flour, stirring, until the dough is the consistency of thick soup or cooked cereal. You may need to add a little more flour. Beat the dough about 100 strokes.

Cover the bowl with plastic wrap and leave in a warm place to double in size—about 1¼ hours.

Uncover the bowl and beat in the baking soda. Let the dough rest while you grease the insides of the rings well with butter or vegetable shortening.

Heat a large, heavy skillet until it is almost smoking, then brush the bottom with vegetable shortening, place the rings inside (you'll probably get four to a skillet), and turn the heat down to very low. Using a ¼-cup measure, ladle a brimming measureful of dough into each ring. The dough will be gooey, like Silly Putty; be sure to scrape it all out with your finger, and after you have poured out each portion of dough, poke it around so that it fills the ring evenly. Bake over low heat, moving the rings a little after the dough has set. After 5 minutes, the surface of the dough should no longer look wet. Remove the rings and turn each muffin with a spatula. Bake for another 5 minutes, then remove the muffins to a rack. Regrease the rings lightly and continue to bake additional muffins in exactly the same way until all the dough is used up. Wrap the English muffins tightly in plastic wrap and store until you are ready to use them.

Just before eating, split each muffin by pulling it apart instead of cutting it. The best way to do this is to poke holes with a fork at even intervals all the way around the edge, then ease the muffin apart with your fingers. Toast the muffin halves in a toaster until lightly browned and spread butter on while they are still hot. Have honey and jam ready.

Buttermilk Pancakes

**Makes one dozen pancakes,
3 to 4 inches in diameter**

*P*ancakes are also a form of bread, cooked by baking in a skillet on top of the stove instead of in the oven. These puff up because of the baking soda in them.

4 tablespoons (½ stick) butter
1 cup buttermilk
1 large egg
1 cup white flour
1 teaspoon baking soda
2 tablespoons sugar
½ teaspoon salt

TOPPING

Butter and warm maple syrup

Put the butter in a small saucepan and melt it over very low heat. Be careful not to let it burn.

Beat together the buttermilk, 2 tablespoons of the melted butter, and the egg in a medium bowl. Mix together thoroughly the flour, baking soda, sugar, and salt in another bowl or on a large piece of waxed paper. Mix the dry ingredients into the liquid, stirring just long enough to moisten the flour. Don't worry if the batter looks lumpy.

Brush the bottom of a large skillet with a little of the remaining butter. Heat the skillet until it is so hot that a drop of water tossed in it will sizzle.

Using a large spoon that holds 2 tablespoons of batter for each cake, scoop up a spoonful of batter and drop it onto one side of the greased skillet or griddle. Drop two more spoonfuls onto other

parts of the skillet to make two more pancakes. Cook for 1 minute or until bubbles begin to appear on the top of each pancake. Turn with a spatula and brown the bottom side—less than a minute. Continue to make batches of pancakes, brushing the skillet lightly with butter each time. Stack the pancakes on a warm plate, cover loosely with foil, and serve immediately when all are done—with lots of butter and warm syrup.

Blueberry Pancakes: When each pancake has cooked on one side and has formed bubbles, sprinkle a few blueberries onto the uncooked side. Turn immediately and cook about 1 minute.

Griddle Scones

Makes sixteen wedges

Scones come from Scotland, and in the old days, cooks there would bake these wedges of rich, currant-studded dough on top of the stove, either in a heavy skillet or on a baking stone. They can also be baked in the oven. They should be eaten still warm from baking with lots of butter and maybe some honey.

2½ cups white flour
2 teaspoons baking powder
½ teaspoon salt
⅓ cup sugar
8 tablespoons (1 stick) butter, cut in small pieces
⅔ cup buttermilk
¾ cup dried currants

Put the flour, baking powder, salt, and sugar in a medium bowl and mix thoroughly. Add the butter, stirring to coat it well with flour, then rub the butter and flour through your fingers. Scoop more pieces of butter up from the bottom, and lifting your fingers above the bowl, rub the fat and dry ingredients together and let them fall back into the bowl. Continue to do this until the mixture resembles oatmeal.

Start slowly heating a heavy nonstick skillet or a baking stone over low heat.

Pour the buttermilk into the flour-butter mixture and stir just enough to moisten the dough. Turn the dough out onto a floured work surface and sprinkle the currants on top, then knead lightly about eight times, giving the dough a quarter turn after each kneading.

Divide the dough in half and pat each half into a circle about 7 inches in diameter.

Cut each circle into eight equal wedges, the way you would cut a cake.

Test your skillet or baking stone by holding your hand an inch above the surface. It should feel warm but not uncomfortably hot.

Arrange the eight wedges of one of the rounds of dough on the pan, leaving a little space between wedges but keeping the pieces in a circle. Bake for about 7 minutes on the first side, lifting with a spatula now and then to make sure they are not browning too quickly on the bottom; if they look too dark, lower the heat. Turn each wedge and bake another 7 minutes on the other side. Now, using tongs or a fork, turn each wedge on its side and bake for 1 minute to crisp the edges, then turn onto the other side and bake a final minute. Remove from the pan and bake the other eight wedges in the same way. Serve warm.

Blueberry-Orange Bread

Makes one 9-inch loaf

*B*reads made with baking powder or baking soda are often called "quick breads"—you don't have to knead them or wait for the dough to rise. They have a more cakelike texture than yeast breads, but are apt to dry out faster. That's why fruits are often added, and sometimes vegetables. Contrasting flavors are this loaf's tangy secret.

3 cups white flour
4½ teaspoons baking powder
¼ teaspoon baking soda
1½ teaspoons salt
½ cup sugar
1 cup blueberries, preferably fresh
1 large egg
1 cup milk
⅓ cup orange juice
1 tablespoon grated orange rind (see box, page 51)
½ cup vegetable oil

Preheat the oven to 350 degrees.

Mix together thoroughly the flour, baking powder, baking soda, salt, and sugar in a large bowl. Toss in the blueberries, and stir them around with your hand to coat them with the flour.

Crack the egg into another bowl, beat it lightly with a fork, then stir in the milk, orange juice, orange rind, and oil. Combine this liquid with the flour mixture, stirring just enough to moisten all the dry ingredients.

Oil a 9-inch loaf pan, pour the batter into it, and bake in the middle of the preheated oven for 1 hour and 10 minutes. The top should be browned and the bread will probably have a crack on top. To be sure it is done, insert a toothpick in the center—it should come out clean. Cool the loaf in the pan for 5 minutes. Run a knife around the edges of the pan to loosen the bread, then turn it out onto a rack to cool thoroughly before slicing.

Quick Breads ■ Muffins

Pumpkin Bread

Makes two 8-inch loaves

*C*innamon and nutmeg fill this pumpkin bread with spice. It has a nice orange color.

3½   cups white flour
1   teaspoon salt
2½   cups sugar
2   teaspoons baking soda
2   cups canned or fresh pumpkin puree (unsweetened and not spiced)
1   cup vegetable oil
½   cup water
4   large eggs, beaten
¾   teaspoon ground cinnamon
½   teaspoon ground nutmeg, freshly grated if possible (see box)
1   cup chopped hazelnuts or walnuts (see box, page 95)

Preheat the oven to 350 degrees.

Mix together thoroughly the flour, salt, sugar, and baking soda on a large piece of waxed paper.

Put the pumpkin, oil, water, eggs, cinnamon, and nutmeg in a large bowl and beat with a whisk or egg beater. Now pour the dry ingredients on the waxed paper into the bowl, mixing only enough to moisten the dry ingredients. Stir in the chopped nuts.

Lightly oil the insides of two 8-inch loaf pans and pour equal amounts of batter into the pans. Bake 50 minutes to 1 hour in the middle of the preheated oven, or until a toothpick inserted in the center of the loaves comes out clean.

Remove from the oven and let the bread cool in the pans for 10 minutes. Run a knife around the edges of the pan to loosen the sides, as illustrated on page 89, and turn the loaves out onto racks to cool.

The Secret of Nutmeg

Nutmeg is a wonderful-tasting spice with a delicate woodsy flavor. The trouble is that once it has been ground and put in a bottle, it loses its flavor and aroma quickly and tastes more like sawdust. The trick is to buy a jar of whole nutmegs, which look like good-sized nuts, and then to grate just the amount you need on the side of the grater with the smallest holes. One nutmeg will yield about 2 teaspoons ground.

Banana-Carrot Bread

Makes one 8-inch loaf

𝓑anana bread is a great bread to make when you have black-spotted bananas that are too squishy to eat, and combined with carrots, the color and flavor are wonderful.

4	tablespoons (½ stick) butter, at room temperature
¾	cup sugar
2	large eggs
2	very ripe bananas
2	cups white flour
½	teaspoon salt
2	teaspoons baking powder
¼	teaspoon baking soda
½	teaspoon ground cinnamon
⅛	teaspoon ground cloves
1	cup chopped walnuts (see box, page 95)
2	medium carrots, peeled and grated (see box)
1	teaspoon vanilla

Preheat the oven to 350 degrees.

Cream the butter by mashing it with a large wooden spoon against the sides of a large mixing bowl until creamy. Add the sugar and beat to mix in as thoroughly as you can. Add the eggs, one at a time, beating well. Use a fork to mash the bananas against a flat plate, and then stir them in.

Mix together thoroughly the flour, salt, baking powder, baking soda, cinnamon, and cloves on a large piece of waxed paper. Make a funnel of the paper and add this dry mixture to the butter-egg-banana mixture, stirring.

Stir in the walnuts, grated carrots, and vanilla, and mix the batter very well.

Butter the inside of an 8-inch loaf pan and pour the batter into it.

Bake in the middle of the preheated oven for 1 hour. The top should be browned and the bread will probably have a crack on top. To be sure it is done, insert a toothpick in the center—it should come out clean.

Allow the bread to cool in the pan for 15 minutes. Loosen the sides by running a knife around the edges of the pan and turn the loaf out onto a rack, as illustrated on page 89. Cool completely before serving.

Peeling and Grating Carrots

Use a vegetable peeler to remove the peel from a carrot. Hold the carrot at the stem end and shave down with the peeler. Repeat, going around the carrot until all the skin is peeled away.

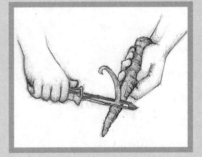

To grate the carrot, rub it against the side of the grater with the coarse holes, holding it at the stem end. Continue until you are down to the nub of the stem. Then stop—or you'll grate your fingers.

Zucchini Bread

Makes one 9-inch loaf

*E*very garden seems to be overflowing with zucchini in midsummer. Here is a way of using up some of the excess. In fact, the bread is so good you could easily double the recipe and put one loaf away in the freezer to eat on a cold, bleak winter day, to remind you of summer.

1½ cups white flour
¾ cup sugar
1½ teaspoons baking powder
½ teaspoon baking soda
½ teaspoon salt
¼ teaspoon ground ginger
2 large eggs
½ cup vegetable oil
1½ cups coarsely grated zucchini*
1 teaspoon grated lemon rind
1 cup coarsely chopped walnuts

Preheat the oven to 350 degrees.

Mix the flour, sugar, baking powder, baking soda, salt, and ginger together on a big piece of waxed paper.

Put the eggs in a medium bowl and beat them only until the yolks and whites are blended. Add the oil, grated zucchini, and grated lemon rind. Pick up the waxed paper with the dry ingredients and dump them into the bowl. Mix only until lightly blended; don't overmix. Stir in the walnuts.

*Grate zucchini the same way as you would carrots, page 93, but do not peel the zucchini.

Lightly oil the inside of a 9-inch loaf pan. Scrape the batter out of the bowl into the loaf pan. Bake in the middle of the preheated oven for 50 minutes, or until a toothpick inserted in the center comes out clean.

Remove from the oven and let the loaf cool in the pan for 5 minutes. Loosen the sides by running a knife around the edges of the pan and turn the loaf out onto a rack to cool, as illustrated on page 89.

Chopping Nuts

Put the nuts close together on a good-sized chopping board. Holding a large knife at both ends, with one hand on the handle and the other just above the point, position the knife only 1 or 2 inches above the nuts and come down firmly on them. Continue to chop this way, moving the knife around and gathering the nuts toward the center as they disperse. If your knife is too high above the nuts and you come down too heavily on them, you will scatter them all over the place and the dog will gobble up most of the pieces.

Corn Bread

Makes twelve 2-inch squares or about fourteen cornsticks

*I*f your kitchen happens to have cast-iron molds that have forms in the shape of small ears of corn, it is fun to make corn bread in them. You can also make a delicious variation of this recipe by substituting whole wheat flour for the white flour—and tripling the amount of sugar—to produce a fragrant, earthy corn bread.

1   cup yellow cornmeal
1   cup white flour
3   tablespoons sugar
¾   teaspoon salt
4   teaspoons baking powder
2   large eggs
4   tablespoons (½ stick) butter, melted
1   cup milk

Preheat the oven to 425 degrees.

Mix together thoroughly the cornmeal, flour, sugar, salt, and baking powder in a medium bowl. In another bowl, lightly beat the eggs and stir in the melted butter and milk.

Mix the liquid ingredients with the dry and beat about 1 minute.

Butter the inside of an 8-inch square baking pan or cast-iron cornstick molds, pour in the batter, and bake in the preheated oven for 25 minutes—20 minutes for the cornsticks. Cut the corn bread into 2-inch squares in the pan, then remove them with a spatula. Or turn out the cornsticks, loosening the sides with a knife if necessary. Serve warm.

Cousin Ed's Irish Soda Bread

Makes one round loaf

*I*n Ireland, the daily ritual called "teatime" is never considered complete without a loaf of traditional soda bread studded with raisins and snowy with a sprinkling of powdered sugar.

2 cups white flour
2 teaspoons baking soda
2 teaspoons baking powder
1 teaspoon salt
3 tablespoons sugar
3 tablespoons butter
1 cup buttermilk
½ cup raisins
2 teaspoons caraway seeds

TOPPING
Confectioners' sugar

Preheat the oven to 375 degrees.

Mix together thoroughly the flour, baking soda, baking powder, salt, and sugar in a medium bowl.

Using two knives (to avoid softening the butter with warm hands), cut the butter into the dry mixture until it consists of pea-sized bits.

Add the buttermilk, raisins, and caraway seeds, and mix just until the dry ingredients are moist.

Gather the dough quickly into a ball and place it on a floured surface. Knead lightly for 1 minute (don't press the dough hard into your work surface as you knead because it will be quite moist). Gather the dough into a ball again and pat down the sides to form a round loaf. Place the round on an ungreased baking sheet.

Dip a sharp knife into flour and use it to cut a large cross 1½ inches deep into the top of the loaf. Sprinkle confectioners' sugar all over the top.

Place the baking sheet in the middle of the preheated oven and bake for 35 minutes, or until the bread is nicely browned on top.

Grandma McLeod's Gingerbread

Makes about eight servings

*G*ingerbread isn't just for dessert. It's wonderful for lunch, split into slices and spread with cream cheese.

¼ cup vegetable shortening

½ cup sugar

¾ teaspoon baking soda

½ cup molasses

1½ cups white flour

¾ teaspoon baking powder

1 teaspoon ground cinnamon

1 teaspoon ground ginger

¼ teaspoon ground cloves

⅛ teaspoon salt

¾ cup boiling water

1 large egg, beaten

TOPPING

Whipped cream or sweet
   butter (optional)

Preheat the oven to 325 degrees.

Cream the shortening by mashing it with a wooden spoon against the sides of a large mixing bowl until creamy. Add the sugar and beat to mix as thoroughly as you can. Put ½ teaspoon of the baking soda and the molasses in a small bowl and, using either an electric or hand-held beater, beat until the molasses becomes light and fluffy, then mix this into the shortening and sugar.

Mix together thoroughly the flour, baking powder, cinnamon, ginger, cloves, and salt on a large piece of waxed paper.

Stir together the boiling water and the remaining ¼ teaspoon baking soda. Gradually add about one-third of this to the shortening-molasses mixture in the bowl, then add about one-third of the dry ingredients. Continue, adding one-third of the water-and-baking-soda mixture, followed by one-third of the dry ingredients, until both have been mixed in. Now add the beaten egg and stir the batter thoroughly.

Grease an 8-inch square baking pan. Sprinkle a little flour over the bottom and sides, then turn the pan over and tap it lightly to get rid of any excess flour.

Pour the gingerbread batter into the pan. Bake for about 25 minutes in the middle of the preheated oven, or until a toothpick inserted in the center comes out clean.

Take the pan out of the oven and cut the gingerbread into squares, then remove the squares from the pan with a spatula. Serve still warm with plenty of whipped cream, if you like that, or simply spread with sweet butter.

Blueberry Muffins

Makes eight to ten muffins

*R*ipe and juicy blueberries make nice, gooey muffins. You can use fresh or frozen berries, or blackberries or raspberries, if they are in season.

1	cup blueberries
2	cups white flour
1	tablespoon baking powder
1	tablespoon sugar
½	teaspoon salt
1	large egg
¼	cup milk
2	tablespoons butter, melted

Preheat the oven to 375 degrees.

Wash the blueberries and shake dry in a strainer. Spread ½ cup of the flour on waxed paper and toss the blueberries in the flour to coat lightly.

Mix together thoroughly the remaining 1½ cups flour, the baking powder, sugar, and salt in a medium bowl or on a sheet of waxed paper. In another medium bowl, beat the egg lightly, then stir in the milk and melted butter. Add the blueberries and the flour mixture, mixing just enough to moisten the dry ingredients. Don't worry if the batter looks lumpy.

Quick Breads ■ *Muffins*

Butter a muffin pan liberally, and pour the batter into the muffin cups to fill them about two-thirds full.

Pop into the middle of the preheated oven and bake for 20 to 25 minutes. After 20 minutes, check to see if the muffins have turned golden brown and have shrunk a little away from the sides of their cups. If not, bake 4 to 5 minutes more.

Run the flat side of a knife vertically around the sides of each muffin cup, and turn the muffins out onto a rack. They should fall out easily. Serve hot with lots of butter.

Quick Breads ■ Muffins

Apple Muffins

Makes ten to twelve good-sized muffins

*B*e sure to use tart, firm apples—
not a soft type like McIntosh—so that the pieces hold their shape.

1	large egg
¼	cup vegetable oil
½	cup light brown sugar
2½	cups white flour
½	cup stone-ground whole wheat flour
4	teaspoons baking powder
½	teaspoon salt
1	cup milk
2	medium apples, peeled, cored, and cut in small dice (see box)

TOPPING

2	teaspoons sugar mixed with ½ teaspoon ground cinnamon

Preheat the oven to 375 degrees.

Beat the egg in a medium bowl, and then add the oil and sugar, continuing to beat until well blended. Mix together thoroughly the white flour, whole wheat flour, baking powder, and salt in another bowl or on a piece of waxed paper. Add the dry ingredients to the egg mixture, then pour in the milk. Fold in the diced apples.

Rub a muffin pan liberally with butter and spoon the batter into the cups, filling them two-thirds full. Sprinkle the topping evenly over all the muffins and bake in the middle of the preheated oven for 20 minutes, or until lightly browned. Remove from the oven and run the flat side of a knife vertically around the sides of each cup. Turn the pan upside down, tapping it to dislodge the muffins. Serve warm.

Quick Breads ■ *Muffins*

How to Prepare Apples

Stand the apples on a cutting board. With a good-sized knife, cut through the stem end to the bottom of each apple, slicing it in half. Put the halves on the board, cut side down, and slice each one in half again.

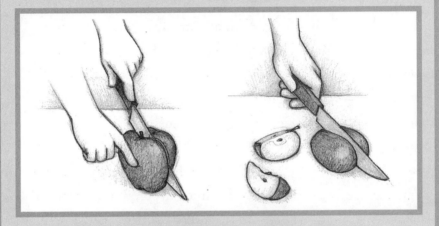

Now, using a small paring knife, peel the quarters and cut out the cores. Slice the apples and then chop them into small pieces, if that is what the recipe calls for.

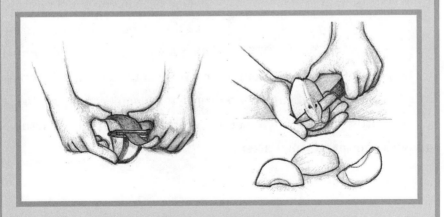

Bacon and Peanut Butter Muffins

Makes twelve muffins

*T*wo all-time favorite ingredients make these muffins delicious any time of day.

2 cups white flour
1 tablespoon baking powder
1 tablespoon sugar
1 teaspoon salt
1 large egg
1 cup milk
2 tablespoons bacon fat or
   butter, melted
3 strips bacon, finely chopped
About 4 tablespoons peanut
   butter

Preheat the oven to 400 degrees.

Mix together thoroughly the flour, baking powder, sugar, and salt on a large piece of waxed paper.

Beat the egg in a medium bowl, then add the milk, melted fat or butter, and chopped raw bacon. Stir in the flour mixture, but do not beat; the dry ingredients should be just moistened.

Grease muffin pans—enough for twelve muffins—and spoon a little batter into each cup. Then drop 1 teaspoon (⅓ tablespoon) of peanut butter into each one before filling the cups three-fourths full with the remaining batter.

Bake in the middle of the preheated oven for 20 to 25 minutes, or until the muffins are lightly browned and shrinking slightly from the sides of the cups. Remove the pans from the oven, tapping them to dislodge the muffins. If necessary, run the flat side of a knife vertically around the sides of the cups to loosen the muffins. Serve warm.

Baking Powder Biscuits

Makes about sixteen biscuits

*T*hese biscuits are very easy and quick to make, and they look so impressive piled in a basket. They are delicious eaten warm with butter and honey or jam. They are also the foundation for that delicious summer dessert, strawberry shortcake—or peach or raspberry, depending on the season. All you do is split the biscuits, spread the bottom halves with sliced berries or fruit, and cover the fruit with the top halves and a generous scoop of sweetened whipped cream. What could be more satisfying on a summer day?

2	cups white flour
2	teaspoons baking powder
½	teaspoon salt
½	cup vegetable shortening
⅔	cup milk

Preheat the oven to 450 degrees.

Put the flour, baking powder, and salt in a large bowl and toss with your fingers to mix well. Add the vegetable shortening, turning it in the flour to coat, then break it into smaller pieces. Now plunge your hands down into the bottom of the bowl and lightly rub pieces of shortening and flour together between your thumb and fingers, bringing your hands up above the rim of the bowl and letting the rubbed pieces fall back in. Continue to do this about forty times, always reaching to the bottom of the bowl to scoop up the flour and aiming for the larger pieces of fat to incorporate. When most of the particles of shortening have been reduced to very small pieces—anywhere in size from a grain of rice to a piece of oat-meal—and are all coated with flour, you will know you have worked the dough enough.

Add the milk all at once and stir with a fork to mix. Now turn the dough out onto a lightly floured work surface and knead it gently about a dozen times.

Pat the dough out with the palms of your hands to a rough cir-cle about 7 inches in diameter. Using a 2-inch round cookie cutter or the rim of a glass that size, cut quickly and firmly into the dough. The round you have cut will probably stick to your cutter, so just give it a good shake and the biscuit will drop. Place it on an ungreased baking sheet. Continue forming the rest of the biscuits and arrange them on the baking sheet, leaving space between. When you have cut as many biscuits as you can from the circle, scoop up the scraps of dough, pat them into a smaller round, and continue cutting out biscuits until all the dough is used up.

Bake the biscuits in the middle of the preheated oven for 12 to 14 minutes. You will know they are done when they have puffed up and turned golden. Eat warm from the oven.

Popovers

Makes eight popovers

$\mathcal{H}$ere is an example of a "bread"—
at least it's served as a bread, piping hot from the oven—that
rises on egg power alone. No yeast, baking powder, or soda is used
as a leavener. It is simply the exposure of the eggs to heat that

makes a popover pop, rising well above its container, usually at a jaunty, lopsided angle. There used to be a lot of theories about how to make popovers—the muffin tins had to be red hot before the popover batter could be poured into them (cast iron was thought to be best), and the butter had to be already sizzling in them. But the truth is that popovers rise just as spectacularly when started in a cold oven and that Pyrex cups are far better than muffin pans because the glass generates so much heat. If you have an oven that can be set to turn on by itself at a specified time, prepare the batter the night before, put it in well-greased Pyrex cups, set the timer, and, lo and behold, everyone will think you have wrought a miracle when you bring on crisp, golden, sky-high popovers for breakfast.

1	cup white flour
½	teaspoon salt
3	large eggs
2	tablespoons butter, melted
1	cup milk

If you have a blender or food processor, dump all the ingredients into its container. Blend until thoroughly mixed, scraping down any flour clinging to the sides. Or put the flour and salt in a bowl, make a well in the center, and add the rest of the ingredients, beating until smooth.

Do no preheat the oven. Pour the batter into eight well-greased 5-ounce Pyrex cups so they are between half and two-thirds full. Place the cups on a baking sheet, leaving space between each cup, and put the baking sheet in a cold oven. Turn the heat to 400 degrees and bake for 35 minutes. Run a knife around the insides of the cups to loosen the popovers, and serve immediately with lots of butter and jam.

Dinner Rolls

Makes twenty-four to thirty rolls

*R*olls are particularly fun to make because their character is changed by the shape you give them. They can be nestled close together in a cake pan, which makes for softer rolls, or you can set them apart on a baking sheet so that the surface becomes more crisp all around. You can make pocketbook shapes, twists, knots, or cloverleafs. And you can sprinkle any of these rolls with poppy, caraway, or sesame seeds just before they're baked.

1 cup milk

2 tablespoons butter

1 tablespoon sugar (white or light brown)

1 teaspoon salt

2 teaspoons active dry yeast

2 tablespoons warm water

2½ - 3 cups white flour

Melted butter

GLAZE

1 egg beaten with
    1 teaspoon water

OPTIONAL TOPPING

Poppy, caraway, or sesame seeds

Heat the milk in a medium saucepan and add the butter, sugar, and salt. Stir to dissolve and set aside to cool.

Put the yeast in a medium bowl and pour the warm water over it. After a minute stir with your finger to dissolve.

Test the milk mixture with your finger to be sure that it is lukewarm, then add it to the yeast. Stir in about 2½ cups of the flour, a cup at a time, until the dough becomes hard to stir.

Turn the dough out onto a floured work surface and cover lightly while you clean out the bowl.

Scrape up the dough and knead, adding more flour as necessary, for 8 to 10 minutes, until smooth and springy.

Butter the inside of the cleaned bowl and return the dough to it, turning to coat. Cover with plastic wrap and let rise until doubled in size—about 1½ hours.

Punch the risen dough down and turn it out onto the floured surface. Form into any of the following shapes:

Round Rolls: Pull off pieces of dough slightly larger than a golf ball. Lightly flour your hands, flatten the ball slightly, and then, using your cupped hands, ease the sides of the dough down and under, at the same time plumping up the ball and taking care that you stretch the elastic skin without breaking it. Pinch together the folds of the dough where they meet on the bottom.

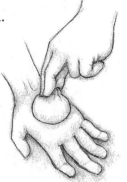

For soft rolls, place side by side in two greased 8-inch cake pans and brush with melted butter.

For crisper rolls, set 1 inch apart on greased baking sheets and brush with the egg glaze. (*continued on page 114*)

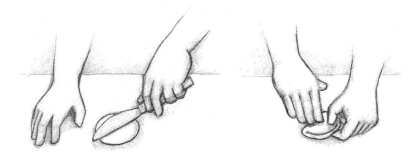

Parker House or Pocketbook Rolls: Pull off pieces of dough large enough to make balls about 2½ inches in diameter. Flatten these into trim circles and then turn them over so that the neater side faces up. Now make a crease down the middle of each with the edge of the dull side of a floured spatula. Brush melted butter over one half and fold the other half over, pressing the edges together securely. Set on greased baking sheets 1 inch or more apart. Brush with the egg glaze.

Cloverleaf Rolls: Make very small balls—half the size of a golf ball—and place three together in the greased cup of a muffin pan, tucking them in so that they nestle close together. Continue until all the dough is used up. You will probably have enough dough for two dozen rolls, so if you don't have enough muffin pans, prepare and bake the cloverleaf rolls in two or three batches. You can also use greased custard cups. Brush the rolls with the egg glaze.

Rolls ■ Buns

Twists: Pull off pieces of dough and roll them into ropes ½ inch in diameter and 6 inches long. Take two strands and pinch the ends together securely, then twist one strand over the other; pinch the ends together at the other end. Place on greased baking sheets 1 inch apart. Brush with egg glaze.

Knots: Pull off pieces of dough and roll them into ropes about ½ inch in diameter and 7 to 8 inches long. Tie the ends of each rope together in a knot. Place on greased baking sheets 1 inch apart. Brush with egg glaze.

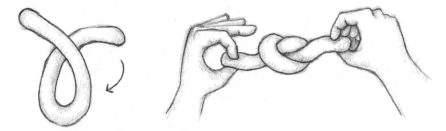

Allow the formed rolls to rise, lightly covered with waxed paper, in a warm place for 40 minutes.

After the rolls have risen for 25 minutes, preheat the oven to 375 degrees. Paint the rolls again with the egg glaze—except for the soft ones in the cake pans. Sprinkle on seeds if you wish.

Bake them in the preheated oven for about 25 minutes or until golden. Remove from the pans and serve warm.

Sticky Buns

Makes 24 buns

*T*hese are known as sticky buns because they bake nestled together on a pool of caramel (butter and brown sugar), so when you pull them apart to eat them, your fingers will be all gooey and sticky. Just lick them off—that's the best part.

Put the yeast in a cup and pour the warm water over it. Stir with your finger to make sure it has dissolved.

Break up the vegetable shortening into several pieces, put them in a bowl, and pour the hot water over. Stir until the shortening is melted. Add the dry milk, salt, sugar, and egg, stirring, and finally the dissolved yeast. Beat with a whisk until everything is well blended.

Now start adding the flour, a cup at a time, stirring well

1　package (1 scant tablespoon) active dry yeast
¼　cup warm water
¼　cup vegetable shortening
1　cup hot water
⅓　cup nonfat dry milk
½　teaspoon salt
¼　cup sugar
1　large egg
About 4 cups white flour
12　tablespoons (1½ sticks) butter, at room temperature
2　teaspoons ground cinnamon
1　cup raisins
2　cups dark brown sugar
1　cup pecans (4-ounce package), very coarsely chopped (you want big pieces)
4　tablespoons corn syrup or maple syrup

after each addition. After you have added 3½ cups and the dough is getting hard to stir, stop and let it rest for about 5 minutes. Then, with a big wooden spoon, beat the dough about fifty strokes. Cover the bowl with plastic wrap and let the dough rise until doubled in size—about 1¼ hours.

Sprinkle your work surface liberally with flour, turn the dough out onto it, and knead lightly about 1 minute. Divide the dough in half. Set one half aside and cover it with a kitchen towel. Put the other half on a well-floured large work surface. Pat it out into an oval, then with a rolling pin roll it out to a rectangle 24 by 6 inches. Rub about 2 tablespoons of the soft butter over the surface and sprinkle on 1 teaspoon of the cinnamon, ¼ cup of the raisins, and ½ cup of the brown sugar. Now, starting with the long side facing you, roll the rectangle up tightly.

Roll out the second half of the dough, rub it with 2 tablespoons butter, and sprinkle on the remaining 1 teaspoon cinnamon, ¼ cup of the raisins, and ½ cup of the brown sugar, then roll it up in exactly the same way.

Smear half of the remaining soft butter (4 tablespoons) over the bottom of an 8-inch cake pan, then smear the remaining 4 tablespoons into a second 8-inch pan. Scatter half of the remaining raisins (¼ cup), ½ cup

brown sugar, and ½ cup pecans, then drizzle 2 tablespoons of the corn or maple syrup over everything on the bottom of one pan. Repeat with the second pan.

Now cut the long rolls of filled dough into 2-inch slices and place them side by side, 1 dozen to each pan; the cut sides should be up so that you see the filling. Cover the pans with a kitchen towel and let rise for 30 minutes.

After the sticky buns have risen for 15 minutes, preheat the oven to 375 degrees. Bake in the middle of the preheated oven for 25 minutes, or until golden brown on top. Remove from the oven and let cool in the pans for 5 minutes, then run a knife around the sides of the pans to loosen the rolls and turn them out, bottom side up, onto two serving plates. The tops will have a dark, gooey glaze. If there is any glaze remaining in the pans, just scrape it out onto the tops of the sticky buns. Eat warm.

Hot Cross Buns

Makes twenty buns

*L*ong ago, bread dough was often slashed with an X to ward off evil spirits, so it seemed a reasonable thing on Good Friday in England to mark the holiday buns with a symbolic cross.

Heat the milk in a small saucepan just to lukewarm and pour it over the yeast in a cup.

Mix 3½ cups of the flour with the salt, sugar, and spices in a large, warm bowl. Make a well in the center and pour in the dissolved yeast. Stir with a big wooden spoon, then stir in the eggs, one at a time; beat in the softened butter. Add a little more flour if necessary to make a firm dough.

Turn the dough out onto a floured work surface and spread it out. Sprinkle the currants over, then fold up the dough and knead a little to distribute them evenly through the dough. (*continued on page 120*)

¾   cup milk

2   packages (2 scant tablespoons) active dry yeast

3½ - 3¾ cups white flour

2   teaspoons salt

2   tablespoons light brown sugar

1   teaspoon ground cinnamon

¾   teaspoon freshly grated nutmeg (see page 91)

¼   teaspoon ground allspice

¼   teaspoon ground cloves

2   large eggs

2   tablespoons butter, softened

½   cup dried currants

OPTIONAL GLAZE

½   cup confectioners' sugar mixed with 2 teaspoons warm milk

(*continued on page 120*)

Rolls ■ *Buns*

Clean out your bowl and return the dough to it. Cover with plastic wrap and let rise until doubled in size—about 2 hours.

Punch down the risen dough, turn it out onto a floured working surface, and knead briefly—less than 1 minute.

Lightly roll the dough into a long roll and then with a knife cut off twenty even-sized pieces. Shape these into buns by rounding them with your two cupped hands, tucking under the sides and pinching the seams together at the bottom. Grease two baking sheets and place the buns 2 inches apart on them.

Cover the buns lightly with waxed paper and let them rise in a fairly warm place until doubled in size—about 35 minutes.

After the buns have risen for 20 minutes, preheat the oven to 450 degrees. Just before baking, with a pair of scissors make a cross in each bun, snipping once horizontally, once vertically, and cutting quite deep. Put them immediately into the middle of the preheated oven for 10 to 15 minutes and bake until golden.

The cross will have opened up in baking.

Rolls ■ Buns

If you want to emphasize the cross and give a little flavor of sweet frosting, mix the confectioners' sugar and warm milk in a small bowl until smooth. Dip a chopstick or the wrong end of a wooden spoon into the frosting and drizzle a little over the buns after they have cooled a bit, following the lines of the cross.

If you don't eat all the hot cross buns right away, they can be reheated or split and toasted.

Challah

Makes one large braided loaf

*T*his light, airy, braided egg bread can now be found in many supermarkets but is even more delicious when made at home. Because turning on a stove is forbidden on the Jewish Sabbath, it is traditional to bake challah (pronounced as if there were no C—"hallah") on Thursday or Friday so that it is sure to be ready before Friday's sundown, the beginning of the holy day. At the Sabbath table the head of the family removes the cloth that covers the bread and says a blessing before slicing the loaf.

1½ packages (1¼ tablespoons) active dry yeast
1 tablespoon sugar
1 cup warm water
2 teaspoons salt
2 large eggs, lightly beaten
2 tablespoons vegetable oil
3½ - 4 cups white flour
GLAZE
1 egg mixed with ½ teaspoon water
Poppy seeds

In a large bowl dissolve the yeast and sugar in the warm water. After a minute stir the yeast with your finger to make sure it is thoroughly dissolved.

Add the salt, eggs, oil, and as much flour as can be stirred into the liquid, a cup at a time. Then turn the dough out onto a lightly floured work surface and let it rest while you clean out the bowl.

Knead the dough for at least 10 minutes, adding more flour as necessary, until the dough is smooth and bouncy.

Shaped ■ Breads

Oil the inside of the bowl and put the dough in it, turning to coat all over. Cover with plastic wrap and let rise until doubled in size—45 minutes to 1 hour.

Punch the dough down and turn it out on a floured surface. Divide it into two equal portions.

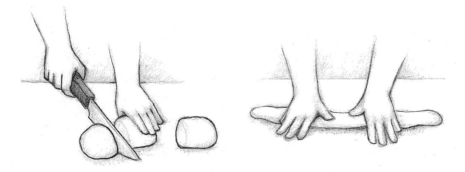

Portion 1: Cut into three equal parts. Roll each part out into a rope 14 to 16 inches long. Line the ropes up side by side in the center of an oiled baking sheet. Pinch the ends together at one end, then braid the three strands and pinch the ends together at the other end.

(*continued on page 124*)

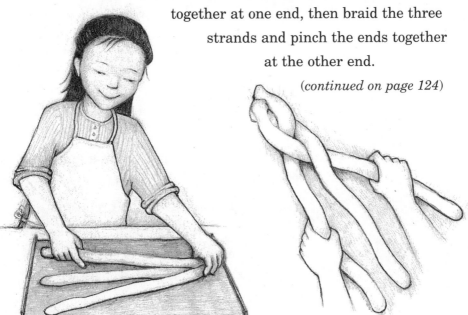

Shaped ■ Breads

Portion 2: Divide into two unequal pieces—the first almost twice the size of the second. Take the larger of the pieces and divide it into three equal parts. Roll these into ropes about 10 inches long and braid them as you did with Portion 1. When you have braided the loaf and pinched the ends, lift the braid and place it on top of the Portion 1 braid.

Now take the smaller piece of Portion 2, divide it into three parts, and roll out ropes about 8 inches long. Braid these and place them on top of the second braid.

Brush with the egg glaze the areas where the braids touch, to help them to adhere. Then lightly cover the whole pile with a floured kitchen towel and let rise until almost double in size—about 40 minutes.

After the challah has risen for 25 minutes, preheat the oven to 400 degrees. Brush the challah all over with the glaze and then sprinkle poppy seeds generously over the top and sides.

Bake in the preheated oven for 10 minutes, then lower the heat to 350 degrees and continue baking for 35 to 40 minutes longer. When the challah has turned golden and shiny, transfer it carefully to a rack and cool.

Shaped ■ Breads

Flowerpot Bread

hy bake bread in a flowerpot? The baked clay that flowerpots are made of is a perfect mold for bread, ensuring a crust that metal bread pans never quite achieve. But first you must season the pots so that the dough won't stick to them.

TREATING THE FLOWERPOTS

Use very clean clay flowerpots and generously rub the insides all over with vegetable oil.

Place the pots in a 450-degree oven and let them bake for 1 hour (do this, if possible, alongside something else that may be baking, so as not to waste fuel).

After this treatment, the pots need simply be washed in warm water after you've baked in them. If you notice any sticking, repeat the treatment.

DOUGHS TO USE

Almost any yeast dough will bake well in a flowerpot, but these are the ones we've found particularly good.

Bubble Bread dough (page 128), using the currants but eliminating the chopped nuts and sticky glaze, and **Sculptured Bread** (page 131). Both of these make nice sweet breakfast breads, particularly when baked in small, individual flowerpots. Sprinkle the tops with sesame or poppy seeds just before baking, or sprinkle powdered sugar over the little breads after baking.

Cheese Bread dough (page 36). This turns beautifully golden and crusty. Sprinkle the tops with grated Parmesan cheese before baking, if you like.

Whole Wheat Bread dough (page 42). This is nice baked in a larger pot so you can slice the bread crosswise for round sandwiches after you've eaten the topknots, which are particularly good if dusted with cracked wheat just before baking.

F o r m i n g   a n d   B a k i n g

Use the dough after it has had its first rising. Punch it down and form it into shapes roughly half the size of the flowerpots you'll be using.

Most flowerpots have a hole in the bottom, so stuff that with a wad of crumpled aluminum foil. Oil the insides of the pots thoroughly, including the bottoms, and have the pots be slightly warm when you put the dough in.

Fill the pots only half full. Clay makes dough expand more readily, so if they are more than half full, the bread will mushroom over the top so much that it will fall over to one side. To make topknots, form rounds of dough the size of golf balls. With your finger, poke a hole in the dough in the pot. Pull one side of each ball of dough to a point, then fit it, point side down, into its hole.

Very small flowerpots will take only one topknot—and in this case the ball should be about half the size of a golf ball; wider pots will take two or three snuggled close together.

$\mathcal{S}$ h a p e d   ■ $\mathcal{B}$ r e a d s

Cover the filled pots with a kitchen towel and let the dough rise until it is almost to the top—about 45 minutes.

After the bread has risen for 30 minutes, preheat the oven to 425 degrees. Just before baking, paint the tops with a glaze of 1 egg beaten with 1 teaspoon water.

Bake in the preheated oven for 15 minutes, then lower the heat to 350 degrees. Small pots will need only an additional 5 to 10 minutes; medium-sized, 10 to 15 minutes; and a large pot, an additional 30 minutes, particularly if you are using whole wheat dough.

Slip the baked breads out of their pots and let them sit a few minutes in the turned-off oven, then cool on racks.

Shaped ■ Breads

Bubble Bread

Makes one 10-inch crown

*H*ere's a bread that's great fun to make, a festive bread to celebrate time off from school. When baked, it looks like a huge royal crown full of gooey bubbles.

2	packages (2 scant tablespoons) active dry yeast
1⅓	cups warm water
⅓	cup nonfat dry milk
½	cup sugar
1	teaspoon salt
4	tablespoons (½ stick) butter, melted
2	large eggs
4½ - 5 cups white flour

GLAZE

1½	cups dark brown sugar
⅓	cup evaporated milk or cream
2	tablespoons corn syrup or maple syrup
5	tablespoons butter
1	cup dried currants
¾	cup chopped pecans

Put the yeast in a large bowl and pour ⅓ cup of the warm water over it. After a minute stir with your finger to make sure that the yeast has dissolved.

Mix the remaining cup of water with the dry milk, sugar, and salt, then pour over the dissolved yeast. Stir in the melted butter (be sure it is only lukewarm). Beat in the eggs, then stir in about 4½ cups of the flour, a cup at a time, until the dough gets hard to stir.

Turn the dough out onto a floured work surface and let it rest while you clean out the bowl.

Scrape up the dough and knead for 6 to 8 minutes, adding more flour as necessary, until it is smooth and bouncy.

Rub the inside of the cleaned bowl with soft butter and return the dough to it, turning to coat. Cover with plastic wrap and let rise in a warm place until doubled in size—about 1 hour.

A few minutes before the rising time is up, prepare the glaze. Put the brown sugar, evaporated milk or cream, corn or maple syrup, and butter into a saucepan and heat until the sugar and butter are dissolved, stirring now and then. Set aside to cool.

Punch the dough down and turn it out onto the floured surface. Tear off pieces of dough the size of golf balls and roll them around in your lightly floured hands to form round bubbles.

After you have formed about ten balls, thoroughly butter a 10-inch cake tube pan (be sure that it does not have a removable bottom or the glaze will leak out) or a Bundt pan. Spread about one-fourth of the glaze over the bottom of the greased tube pan, then sprinkle on one-fourth of the currants and nuts. Now place the

Shaped ■ Breads

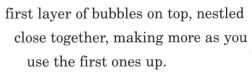

first layer of bubbles on top, nestled close together, making more as you use the first ones up.

On top of this layer drizzle another one-fourth of the glaze, currants, and nuts, and then cover with another layer of bubbles. Repeat until everything has been used, finishing off with glaze on top.

Cover the pan with waxed paper and let rise in a warm place until the bubbles have risen to the top of the pan—about 30 minutes.

After the bread has risen for 15 minutes, preheat the oven to 350 degrees. Bake in the preheated oven for 45 minutes, or until the top of the crown is caramel-colored. Peek after the first half hour to make sure the top isn't turning too dark; if it is, make a tent of aluminum foil and cover.

Remove from the oven and let rest 10 minutes before turning out onto a rack. Serve warm. Everyone just pulls off a gooey "bubble," spreads a bit of butter on it, and eats it up.

Shaped ■ Breads

Sculptured Bread

*B*y using your imagination, you can create your own delightful bread shapes. Use raisins or currants for eyes, strips of orange peel for fins or feathers, strands of thin spaghetti for long whiskers

perhaps, wheat berries or pine nuts for teeth—whatever strikes your fancy.

1	package (1 scant tablespoon) active dry yeast
¼	cup warm water
⅓	cup sugar
2	large eggs
4	tablespoons (½ stick) butter, melted
¼	cup light cream or milk
1	teaspoon vanilla
½	teaspoon salt
1	teaspoon grated orange rind
2½ - 3 cups white flour	
GLAZE	
1	egg mixed with 1 teaspoon water

Put the yeast in a medium bowl and mix with the warm water and sugar. Stir with your finger, and when the yeast has dissolved, add the eggs, butter, cream or milk, vanilla, salt, and orange rind to the yeast and beat until thoroughly mixed. Stir in 2½ cups of the flour, then turn the dough out onto a floured work surface and knead, adding more flour as necessary, until smooth—6 to 7 minutes.

Clean the bowl, rub the inside with softened butter, and return the dough to it, turning to coat. Cover with plastic wrap and leave

in a warm place until doubled in size—1½ to 2 hours (the higher proportion of sugar and eggs will make this dough slower to rise, and it does need a warm place, such as in a turned-off oven with a pilot light or near a radiator).

Turn the dough out and tear off as much of it as you want to work with, covering the remainder with a kitchen towel. If you want to make a long shape, roll your piece out and then flatten it. This dough has a will of its own and may suggest a form to you—perhaps a fish, a bird, a rabbit, a turtle, a snail, or some prehistoric creature. Put the "body" on a greased baking sheet. If you want to make legs or a tail, pinch off a small piece from the remaining dough, roll it into shape, and then attach it to the main body by brushing the edges with glaze, poking a hole in the dough where you want it to go, and then inserting it. Make round balls for ears and noses. Decorate your shapes however you wish.

Cover the shapes lightly with a kitchen towel, and let rise again for 45 minutes, until doubled in size. You will notice how your shapes change and take on a life of their own as the dough swells.

After the bread has risen for 30 minutes, preheat the oven to 350 degrees. Paint the surface of your sculptures with the glaze, and if you want to carve a pattern on the surface, do so with the tip of a sharp knife.

Bake in the preheated oven for 20 to 25 minutes, depending on how thin your sculpture is. Watch carefully, and if some of the extremities seem to be browning too much, cover them with foil.

When the shapes are golden, remove them from the oven. While still warm, lift the shapes off carefully, using one or two spatulas, and let cool on racks.

Crisp Bread Sticks

Makes ten sticks, about 15 inches long

*W*hy does everyone seem to love bread sticks? Perhaps because they look so festive on tables in Italian restaurants arranged in vases like flowers. And they are so delicious to munch on while you are waiting for the main event of a meal. You can eat them right after they are freshly baked, but they turn more crunchy within twenty-four hours and will stay good for several days. In the unlikely event that you have any left, you can freeze them.

1½   teaspoons (½ package) active dry yeast
1   cup warm water
¼   teaspoon salt
2¼ - 2½ cups white flour

GLAZE
1   egg white (see page 39), beaten with 1 teaspoon water

TOPPING
3   tablespoons poppy, sesame, caraway, or fennel seeds
2 - 3 tablespoons coarse salt, kosher or sea salt

Put the yeast in a medium bowl and pour the warm water over it. After a minute stir with your finger to make sure the yeast is dissolved.

Stir in the salt and 2 cups or a little more of the flour to make a fairly stiff dough. Turn it out onto a floured surface and let it rest while you clean the bowl.

Knead the dough, adding more flour as necessary, until it is smooth and elastic—8 to 10 minutes. Return it to the cleaned bowl, cover with plastic wrap, and let rise until tripled in size—2 to 2½ hours.

Punch the dough down and let it rise again for 30 minutes.

Turn the dough out onto a large, lightly floured work surface and divide it into ten equal pieces. One by one, start rolling each piece out, placing your flattened hands in the center of the dough and moving them slowly outward, rolling as you go. Try to keep the thickness of the rolls as even as possible. When each one is about 15 inches long, let it hang from your hand for a second to keep its length, because it will want to pull back. Place on baking sheets several inches apart. Cover with kitchen towels and let sit 30 minutes.

After the sticks have risen for 10 minutes, preheat the oven to 450 degrees, lined with a baking stone or tiles if possible (see page 65). Heat a kettle of water, and when it is boiling, open the oven door and set a large, shallow pan at the edge, then carefully pour about 1 inch of the boiling water into it and slide the pan gently onto the oven floor. The boiling water, which will create steam that makes the bread sticks brown and crispy, should go in about 15 minutes before you are ready to bake.

Paint the top of each stick with the egg white glaze. Sprinkle on whatever seeds you want to use

Shaped ■ Breads

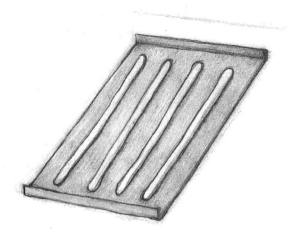

and then distribute coarse salt on top. Sometimes it is fun to decorate two sticks with one kind of seed, two sticks with another kind, and so on, leaving two plain so you have an array of different flavors.

Bake for 15 minutes, then take a look and see if the sticks are nicely browned. If not, bake them another minute or two. Carefully lift the sticks from the pan, gently prying loose with a spatula any stuck areas where the glaze has dripped. Prop up the sticks so air circulates as they cool.

Pretzels

Makes about twenty pretzels

*P*retzels are great fun to make. And no matter how diligently you follow these directions, each one is going to have a slightly different shape and a character of its own.

Put the yeast in a large bowl and pour ¼ cup of the warm water over it. Stir with your finger until the yeast is dissolved. Stir in the remaining water and the brown sugar. Gradually add most of the flour, stirring vigorously, until the dough holds together.

1	package (1 scant tablespoon) active dry yeast
1½	cups warm water
⅓	cup dark brown sugar
About 3½ cups white flour	
2 - 3 tablespoons kosher salt	
6 - 8 tablespoons baking soda	

Turn the dough out onto a floured work surface and knead it, adding more flour as necessary, for about 5 minutes. Cover the dough with a kitchen towel.

Grease two baking sheets and sprinkle a thin layer of coarse kosher salt over the surface. Fill a large frying pan with water, taking note of how many cups it takes to fill it and adding 1 tablespoon baking soda per cup. Let the water come slowly to a boil as you form the pretzels and preheat the oven to 475 degrees.

Now pinch off pieces of dough the size of golf balls. Roll each one out on your floured work surface using the palms of your hands, starting at the center and working outward, until the

Shaped ■ Breads

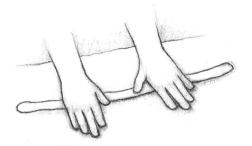 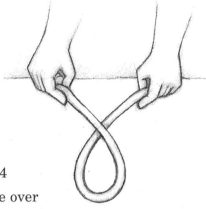

dough has been stretched to a rope 14 inches long. Cross one end of the rope over the other, leaving 3 inches from the crossing point to the tips. Now twist the crossed ends, making a full turn, and bring the tips down onto the U-shape, pressing them firmly

into the dough. With your finger, open up any holes that seem tight, so that you have a good pretzel shape. As each pretzel is formed, put it on a lightly floured tray.

The water should now be boiling gently. With a spatula pick up a pretzel and gently lower it into the water, adding another quickly until you have about six in the pan; they should not be touching. When they are all in, count slowly to 30, then with a spatula lift each pretzel out of the water, starting with the first one. Pat it dry with a paper towel, then flip it over onto the greased and salted baking sheet. When you have filled the baking sheets (the pretzels should not be touching), pop them into the oven and bake for 8 minutes until golden brown.

■ Index ■

▪ About the Authors ▪

Judith and Evan Jones have been baking bread with children since one of their daughters came home from a sculpting class and began working with dough as if it were modeling clay. It is the fun of making bread that is the basis of all the recipes in this book, and each of the breads here has been tested by beginning cooks.

Judith Jones, an editor at Alfred A. Knopf in New York, learned to cook in her aunt's Vermont kitchen. Her husband, the late Evan Jones, began cooking as a youngster in Minnesota and is the author of books of history that include *American Food: The Gastronomic Story* and *The World of Cheese*. They collaborated on *The Book of Bread,* published in 1982, and The *L. L. Bean Book of New New England Cookery*, published in 1987.